# The way I saw it.

The Wyse Advertising lobby on the fourth floor at 2800 Euclid welcomed visitors with weathered barn-wood walls that were adeptly appointed with antique advertising posters and artifacts from the 19th and early 20th centuries.

# The way I saw it.

## Marc Wyse

### with Christopher Johnston

iUniverse, Inc.
Bloomington

## The Way I Saw It.

iUniverse books may be ordered through booksellers or by contacting:

iUniverse
1663 Liberty Drive
Bloomington, IN 47403
www.iuniverse.com
1-800-Authors (1-800-288-4677)

ISBN: 978-1-4759-2419-0 (sc)
ISBN: 978-1-4759-2420-6 (hc)
ISBN: 978-1-4759-2421-3 (e)

Library of Congress Control Number: 2012909686

Printed in the United States of America

iUniverse rev. date: 2/7/2013

# DEDICATION

I dedicate this book to my wife Sheila, my daughter Jennifer, and to those family and friends who remained by my side following my massive stroke in 2005 and taught me about the power and goodness of unconditional love.

# Table of Contents

# Foreword

If you're reading this book, you know my father as Mr. Marc Wyse, "Cleveland's Guru of Advertising." Maybe you're a budding entrepreneur looking for inspiration. Maybe you're a seasoned executive curious about the business strategies of one of your peers. Maybe you're not an advertising person at all, and you just want to know what the "Mad Men" era was *really* like. (FYI: If you're looking for reminisces of three-martini lunches and sex scandals, you might want to put this one back on the shelf.) Anyway, before you get engrossed in the rags-to-riches tale of the co-founder of Wyse Advertising, I'd like to give you a peek at the Marc Wyse who I knew: My Dad.

My Dad is my hero. Always has been, always will be. I used to call him "the giant." As a kid, I would be talking with my mom after school and hear Dad's footsteps pounding up the stairs as he came home from work. I would squeal, "It's the giant!" and Dad would come in and give us bear hugs. At six foot two, he was a big guy. But Dad was a giant to me because of who he was as a man.

I remember Dad working on this book more than fifteen years ago, when I was in sixth grade. He sat at his desk on the weekends and hand wrote it in pen. I'm not sure I know anyone else who is that confident to write their biography in pen. But, after almost fifty years in the advertising business, Dad knew he had a remarkable story to tell. It's the story of the American dream come true. Dad was a first-generation American who worked hard for success and actually found it. Of course, if he had not had a knee injury and had joined his friends fighting in World War II, I probably wouldn't be here, and you wouldn't be reading this book. Good luck, combined with his perseverance, warmth and creativity, allowed his life to unfold as it did.

My father prided himself on his writing skills and broad vocabulary and encouraged me to write as much as I could. When I was barely eight years old, he was teaching me words like "ubiquitous" and "soporific." Unsurprisingly, the way he taught me the word was to put it in a sentence related to a product. "Coca-Cola is ubiquitous." Or, with a smile, he'd say, "*Smucker's* is ubiquitous." I also watched "Jeopardy" with Dad from a very young age. When I was a toddler and the contestant got a "double Jeopardy," I would jump up and down and squeal, "Double bee, double bee!"

As I grew older, we tried to guess the answers before the contestants did. By the time I was a senior in high school, I knew many of the answers on the "College Jeopardy" show, and Dad and I were going head to head. It was our weekday dinnertime entertainment and our quality time together. Dad's encouragement for me to study and write paid off: I have since received my liberal arts degree from Barnard College and dabbled in some writing jobs. Dad beamed with pride when I interviewed Estée Lauder Executive Evelyn Lauder for *COSMO girl!* magazine. He framed the article for me as a gift with the caption "Jennifer's First Nationally Published Work." His next bit of advice was for me to start pitching pieces for *The New York Times*. There was no glass ceiling for Dad, not for his clients or for me; anything was possible.

As far as Dad was concerned, there was nothing to fear in this world. When I was only eighteen weeks old, we went on our first family trip to Hawaii. He was so anxious for me to experience the joy of swimming that he scooped me up and brought me right up to the shore of the Pacific. A massive wave crashed into us, and I immediately began to bawl, salt water and tears streaming down my face. Dad carried me back to the lounge chair and recounted to my mother with laughter that I was a natural swimmer. Admittedly, it is a little unorthodox to take an infant on a trip halfway around the world and then test their swimming skills in the largest body of water on earth. But Dad had no fear of taking healthy risks, both in business and parenting. Resistant as I was at first to the water, I was in swim classes only a few months later and zipped around like a fish in our outdoor pool. I learned to love swimming so much that I began to do it competitively.

The only time I saw my father in fear was when I was standing over him in intensive care, after his massive stroke in 2005. In September, Dad was swimming thirty laps every morning, driving downtown to and from work, and managing a multimillion-dollar advertising agency. In October, he found himself in a hospital bed unable to move the left side of his body, swallow or speak. He tried desperately to tell us something, but he could only manage to mumble. I got a pen and paper and asked him to try writing what he wanted to say. Dad scribbled on the page, "This is torture." The man who was always his own boss, the master of his own destiny, was suddenly dependent on others for his mere survival. He seemed terrified, and so was I. The giant had been defeated.

…Or so I thought. My father lived for six long years after his stroke. Even as his body failed, he refused to give up on life. After three months in an inpatient facility, he chose not to go into a nursing home, but to return to his normal life as much as possible. He deeply believed that he would walk again, even in his final months of life. Every time we spoke on the phone, he updated me on how many steps he took in his last physical therapy session. He also kept his passion for work alive. Even from his hospital bed, he pitched ideas for ketchup and coffee brands. He mentored many young entrepreneurs. He and my mother, Sheila, along with the Cleveland Advertising Association, even opened a scholarship fund in Marc's name. And, amongst everything else, he wrote this book. I was truly privileged to witness my father's courage in the face of unimaginable obstacles. When most people would have given up, Dad saw the aftermath of his stroke as just another chapter of his life, and as a second chance to enjoy his last years on this earth.

I know people my age whose parents never taught them how to swim and who fear water. I'm blessed to have a Dad who showed me that I don't have to be afraid of big waves. I can learn how to navigate them, swim above them, and I'll be okay. And I might come out laughing, too.

Jennifer Wyse
New York, New York
January 2012

# 1 They Called Me the Kinsman Cowboy

I don't know about you, but I grew up in a great time and in a great neighborhood. Maybe I say this out of nostalgia all these years later, but if I look at how kids live and play today, I can claim with confidence that ours was a simpler era.

My life in Cleveland began, fittingly, on a Monday, April 9, 1923, when I was born Marcus Allen Weiss. The stork had deposited my brother, Jacob (Jack) Edwin Weiss, almost exactly nine years before me on April 4, 1914. The Weisses lived downstairs in a two-family home at 3645 East 154th Street, just south of Kinsman Avenue in the Kinsman neighborhood. My parents rented from Mr. Wurtzner, who lived upstairs. My window looked at our neighbor's house. I could almost touch it. As sure as sunrise, the milkman placed milk bottles in our milk box, and a local baker regularly dropped off hard rolls or biscuits at our door.

Back then, it was mostly a Jewish and Italian neighborhood, but there was a great mix of ethnicities. My friends came from all different heritages, and a diverse group of neighbors would come over and sit on our big front porch and talk. A bunch of the tough guys from the neighborhood liked to hang out at the bowling alley on the corner of Kinsman and East 154th. Across the street, streetcars would turn around and go back downtown to Public Square.

Even though we didn't have a lot of money, the world overflowed with wonders for an inquisitive boy. We played with guns we made from cut-up inner tubes. We'd take the rubber and use it to project small pieces of wood. If you got hit by one, you had to play dead. I was a pretty good shot. That's why they called me the Kinsman Cowboy.

East 154th was built of bricks and could get quite slippery, but that never stopped us from playing baseball or touch football in the street. Jack owned a football, so all of the kids would come to our house to play. In fact, Jack was always giving us balls or equipment to play sports, as he was very generous in ensuring that his little brother had fun or finding time to coach my friends and me how to play.

Our field of dreams was the extra lot behind our garage on East 156th that was in Shaker Heights and was known as Ritchey's Field, where we spent many hours playing softball or baseball. Like my childhood friend Sydney "Skippy" Friedman always says, "As long as somebody had a bat and a ball, twenty kids could play." We'd watch the adult softball leagues, too, where the guys would wear T-shirts with their sponsors' names, like Comella Sporting Goods or Chase Brass. There was always lots of action. Sometimes they'd get into fights. They were rough guys, but some of them were good athletes. That lot was also where our garbage cans resided. So, I would tell people, yes, I live in Cleveland, but my garbage cans are in Shaker. Of course, sometimes we'd start fires in the big trash cans, because we figured out that if you put a potato on the end of a stick, you could have a scrumptious baked potato snack.

I love swimming, and I've had a thing for swimming pools my whole life. I've had one at almost every one of my homes. I guess my passion for pools all started that day when I was five or six and I decided we needed one in our backyard. I took a shovel and started digging out our grass. Then I put our garden hose into the hole and filled it up. My first pool… would come many years later. This time, all I got was a lot of mud.

I loved cats, too. I thought they were so agile and entertaining to watch. I decided one day to trap and catch all of the cats in our neighborhood. I ended up with fourteen cats in our basement. My mother got very angry, because all of the neighbors were yelling at her, saying, "Your son's got our cat!" But I kept them in the basement in boxes and in the mangle for the sheets until the neighbors came one-by-one and reclaimed them all.

Who needed money? So many easy pleasures all around.

The older I got, the more I treasured the time I shared with my family, too. There was no better way to spend a freezing cold winter's night. We seemed to have more fierce winters then, with snow up to your chest. But our house was always warm. I was the one who went out to get coal from the pile, and then Jack and I would shovel it into the furnace. Then we would all sit around the living room and listen to the radio, mostly classical music.

We had a big kitchen that made a great gathering place. For breakfast, we'd have milk dishes; for dinner, we'd have meat dishes, since they had to be kept separate. We also had to keep the silverware and the plates for each separate. We had another set of each for Passover, when we had to take our everyday silverware and dishes out of the kitchen and replace them with the Passover ware.

Because of all of those wonderful meals where we would talk about what happened in school that day or what games we played, I have always believed the family that eats together stays together. You need to communicate and know what's happening in your family members' lives. I made sure we did it with all of my kids, too.

After dinner, my mother would wash the dishes in the big, deep sink while Jack and I played or drew pictures or did homework at the kitchen table. She was what is known in Yiddish as a "bolabusta." In other words, she knew how to take care of her family and her home. When she cooked or baked, everything was delicious. When she cleaned or decorated, everything was immaculate.

Every Friday for Shabbat, she baked challah bread, and she boiled chicken and carrots with some spices so that she could serve her fresh bread with chicken soup. After dinner, she always cleaned the kitchen floor. Once it dried, she covered it with newspapers to keep it clean. Saturday morning we would go to temple. Then by Saturday night, the papers would usually all be torn and messy, but they kept the floor clean for a day or two.

No matter what we were doing, we just enjoyed being together, gathering around the radio or sharing meals or listening to my father read stories from the Jewish newspaper to my mother. They would laugh or comment on the story, but Jack and I never really understood what they were about, since we didn't know much Hebrew. Throughout their marriage, my parents always spoke Yiddish or Hungarian to each other, which we didn't know, either.

But it was a precious language to these gentle, hard-working European immigrants. Both my parents were born in the fall of 1889 in a small town, Gernyes, near what was then Hurst, Hungary. The borders have since changed hands several times, sometimes Hungary, other times Czechoslovakia or Russia. Their little town in the Sub-Carpathian region of Europe is now known as Kopasnovo, Ukraine.

My father's name was Leib Angelovich. But his name would change, too. He married my mother, Jennie Herskowitz, in Gernyes. They later sailed on the *S.S. Kronprinz Wilhelm*, departing from Bremen, Germany, on November 15, 1910, and docking at the port of New York on November 22.

My father enjoyed telling us the story of what happened to our family name once they arrived at Ellis Island. According to the misspelled passenger list, "Leib Anczilowicz" was a laborer who couldn't read or write (though he did sign his naturalization papers), had paid for the ticket himself, and arrived with a grand total of $28 in his pocket. After waiting in line for what seemed like hours, they finally stepped up to the kind but officious guard at the immigrant processing desk.

"What's your name?" he inquired.

"Leib Angelovich," my father responded.

The guard nodded mechanically and said to them, "See where that white line is? Go stand behind that line."

My mother and father walked over to the line. "Now your name is Weiss," the guard informed them. Weiss, of course, is German for "White." Had they been sent to stand behind the black line, our name would have been Schwartz, which is German for "Black." Thus, when my parents settled in Cleveland, their names were Louis and Jennie Weiss. What a strange, transformative experience it must have been for all of those brave souls journeying to America.

Louis Weiss was the oldest son of seven children. Several of his siblings stayed in Gernyes, and several immigrated to other countries. One brother, Simkha, moved to Budapest, where he married and had six children, and then emigrated from Hungary to Israel in 1947. Sam, who went by Arthur here, came to Cleveland with my father and lived with us for many years. He loved us very much and often gave Jack and me dimes or quarters when we were kids. (Uncle Arthur once financed the construction of my first car: a red wagon that I meticulously added lumber and homemade wheels to, and then fell apart on its maiden voyage down a hill.) Their sister Helen came to Cleveland for a while, but ended up settling in Oakland, California. With unfathomable sorrow, we lost loved ones to the Holocaust. Fortunately, several of our surviving family members immigrated to the U.S. and Cleveland after World War II.

Earlier in the 1900s, a significant number of Jews from Marmaros County, Hungary, had fled other horrors such as pogroms and conscription into the Russian military and sought freedom and a chance to achieve a better life in Cleveland. Together, they organized the Marmaroscher B'nai Jacob Society in the Woodland neighborhood. My father was a member of the self-help, religious society, which later became the Green Road Synagogue. Actually, I now know many of the details about my ancestors and the chain migration at that time thanks to my lovely wife, Sheila, who had my father's family genealogy researched and written as a 70th birthday present for me.

Our last name mutated one more time, when, as an adult, my big brother Jack legally changed his to Wyse, while I was attending Dartmouth College in the mid-'40s. When I returned to Cleveland in 1946, I legally changed my full name to Marc Wyse. It made sense to have the same name as my brother. My mother eventually changed her last name to Wyse, some years after my father died.

In his mid-20s when he got to Cleveland, Louis Weiss, like many immigrants, knew he wanted to start his own business someday. First, however, he needed to secure a decent, regular income to pay for his home, food and family. He had to learn English, even just enough to communicate with his employers. A friend and fellow immigrant from his town in Hungary bought a big truck and started a company called New York Star Moving. Knowing my father was an ideal employee, standing at a husky and strong 5'6" and 200 pounds, he offered him a job. To his surprise, young Mr. Weiss turned it down and instead accepted a job as a dishwasher at Allendorf's Restaurant in downtown Cleveland.

A fast study, my father quickly mastered the art of soup-making, with the training of the chef, who had graciously taken him under his wing. On June 12, 1919, when he filed his Declaration of Intent to become a citizen of the United States in Cleveland's U.S. District Court, he indicated that he was employed as a cook, and that he and my mother were then living at 2308 East 97th Street. Cook wasn't his dream position, though.

Soon, the entrepreneur in him drove Louis to partner with another friend, a Russian immigrant named Janowitz, to open a restaurant and bar at East 9th Street and Superior Avenue in Cleveland. Not too long afterwards, The Fireside Restaurant went bankrupt. My father, who ran the kitchen, believed the primary cause was Janowitz's son, the bartender, who was partial to helping himself to the cash register. Freely and frequently.

Next, despite the Great Depression, my father opened a restaurant at 2027 Superior Avenue in 1934. This time, wisely, he was the sole proprietor and operator. Today, more than 75 years later, the Maltz Museum of Jewish Heritage in Beachwood, an eastern suburb of Cleveland, displays a photograph of Weiss's Restaurant in its permanent collection.

The restaurant served Hungarian and Jewish cuisine. Each day, my father lovingly prepared fresh batches of his tasty lentil or bean soups, while my mother baked her unforgettable pastries, including her famous Delco cookies loaded with sweet fruit or cheese fillings. To this day, we still keep a copy of "Aunt Jennie's Delcos" circulating throughout the family.

Through winter winds or summer swelter, I remember tagging along with my dad at 4:00 am to the Central Market on Woodland Avenue and East 55th Street, which served as the main produce market at that time, to purchase fresh fruits and vegetables for the restaurant. I would help him carry the bushel baskets to the car. Every year, he would buy a new Chevrolet. Every year. I guess that's where I got my love of cars. That and I don't like to walk much.

At the restaurant, I would watch my dad slice and dice all of the fresh vegetables very quickly. When I would try it, he would yell, "Hey, watch your fingers!" He'd say it with a smile. My father always had a big smile on his face.

I also helped bus tables or make sandwiches or assiduously completed any other tasks I could handle. When I got older, I pushed a cart packed with boxed lunches around to the neighboring businesses. At the time, it was Cleveland's garment district, and the offices of *The Plain Dealer*, the city's daily newspaper, were located nearby on Superior, as they are today.

When I wasn't working at the restaurant or playing sports, I was at school. Somehow, though, I managed to find ways to work wherever I was. I guess I had a lot of energy, and I have always enjoyed the sense of accomplishment. When I attended AJ Rickoff Elementary School at East 147th Street and Kinsman Avenue, there was a huge, open front lawn inside of the iron fence that surrounded the school property. So, for gym class, they would give us push mowers, and away we would go. We loved cutting the grass. It was fun.

I moved on to tougher physical and mental challenges at Alexander Hamilton Junior High School at East 130th Street between Union and Kinsman avenues. I wasn't my full height of 6'2" yet, but I was still pretty tall for my age. I grew up playing basketball and had no problem making the varsity squad. Of all the sports I played, basketball was my absolute favorite. I had a lot of other interests, though. Writing was one of them, so I served on our school newspapers throughout junior high and high school.

At Alexander Hamilton, I ended up serving as managing editor of our paper, the *Hamilton Federalist*. Our faculty advisor, Virginia Fallin, was an incredible journalist and mentor. The lessons I learned from her have stayed with me the rest of my life. She taught us how to prepare and conduct productive interviews as well as how to write clean, concise copy that was interesting and informative.

One of my favorite article assignments for her was to interview Ken Keltner, the great and sure-handed third baseman, then in his rookie season for the Cleveland Indians. I had seen many games with Jack at League Park and the new Municipal Stadium, which a lot of people thought was too big for baseball. At the time, the Indians alternated their games between the two facilities. Keltner was the nicest guy and spent a lot of time with me to make sure I had a good interview that ran in our May 13, 1938, issue of the *Hamilton Federalist*. He talked about how he had dreamed of being a Major Leaguer ever since he was 14 and playing sandlot ball in his hometown of Milwaukee, Wisconsin, and then got his start in the minor leagues in 1937 with the Milwaukee Brewers. He predicted that the Indians would finish at the top of the division, but they ended up in third place that year, 13 games behind the dreaded New York Yankees.

Keltner played all but his last season (13 games with the Boston Red Sox) with the Indians, and is most famous for halting the Yankee's future Hall of Famer Joe DiMaggio's Major League record hitting streak at 56 games on July 17, 1941, at Cleveland Municipal Stadium. I was at that game, and witnessed the historic sports moment from behind home plate. Many years later, I met Joltin' Joe at a business event. When I told him I had seen Keltner's great plays that day to snatch up every one of his hard-hit balls, all he said was, "I was there."

By the time I attended John Adams Senior High School, I had reached my full height and was pretty quick on the courts. I played forward on the varsity basketball team for four straight years. Although we never won the East Senate League championship, we had some pretty good teams, and I always loved playing. I loved our coach, too, Ed Kregenow, who was a real gentleman. When we went on dates after games, we could get an ice cream cone at the shop across the street for a nickel and see a movie at the Imperial Theater at East 142$^{nd}$ and Kinsman for a dime.

I wrote for the John Adams *Journal*, the school newspaper, and ended up serving as the managing editor. We had a remarkable journalism teacher and faculty advisor for the paper, Verta Evans. She taught us how to write tight, sensible and comprehensible stories. Under her guidance, when I was the editor, the National Scholastic Press Association named us the best high school newspaper in the country.

When I graduated in June 1941, I won an honor key, the highest award bestowed on seniors and one of only nine given to our class of 545 students for my participation in extracurricular activities, including managing the radio bulletin, co-managing the *Journal*, serving on the Central Committee and lettering in basketball. The honor key also recognized scholarship. Comprehensive IQ testing in 10th grade had placed me in section one, the highest academic level, and I maintained that ranking throughout high school, where I was on the Honor Roll and was a member of the National Honor Society. So that night, I sat in the front row at Cleveland's Public Hall with the other honor key winners. I have many lifelong friends from high school, and we still consider ourselves the best class John Adams ever had.

Of course, my parents were very proud of me. They must have been pleased to see the fruits of their arduous journey to the U.S. and all the hours and the ups and downs of running their own restaurant rewarded. For my part, I knew that I had many bigger things ahead of me, and I was excited by all of the opportunities I anticipated. Quite honestly, though, I had no complaints about my life as the Kinsman Cowboy.

# 2 | Destined to be a Self-Made Man

No one had a more exciting freshman year than we did. Actually, it was the beginning of a rather interesting decade, through which I navigated a circuitous route toward my adult life and my own business. I entered Adelbert College of Western Reserve University in September of 1941. You know what happened in December. I heard it all unfold with my Zeta Beta Tau fraternity brothers, as we huddled around the radio after the Japanese attacked Pearl Harbor on that day of infamy and FDR declared war on Japan and Germany. ZBT was and still is the largest Jewish fraternity in the U.S. I made many lasting friendships there and will never forget sharing that day with my brothers.

That fall, I was taking my core requirement classes, with the intention of declaring English as my major. My father wanted me to be a lawyer. My mother wanted me to be a doctor. I became an advertising executive. Well, not just yet, but I see now that I was moving in that direction. In keeping with my love of writing and journalism, it wasn't long before I joined the school newspaper, *The Reserve Tribune*, and soon became sports editor.

I was acquiring my writing skills first, before moving into sales, and then combining the two to create an advertising business. At first, my parents might have been a little disappointed, as they dreamt of a better life for me. They knew lawyers and doctors made a heck of a lot of money and had excellent job security, but they trusted me and wanted me to pursue my dreams, too.

After we entered World War II, I was not drafted immediately but classified as AERC, Army Enlisted Reserves Corps, and given the rank of army private unassigned. At that time, most college students were told to remain at home until we were called to active duty. Within about a year, my fraternity emptied out as my brothers were called and assigned to different training camps, where they drilled and prepared before being sent overseas. Several went into the U.S. Army, the Army Air Corps or the U.S. Naval Reserve.

Several never came back. Bob Levine from Springfield, Ohio, was one of them. Great guy. One of the nicest I ever knew, and very handsome. All the girls were crazy about Bob. He became a B-29 pilot, and then on a mission over Germany, his plane was hit by flak and crashed. Arnie Feinberg, another pilot and one of my closest friends in ZBT, became extremely ill and died while serving in Europe. During the war, I corresponded with all of my fraternity brothers serving in the military, and I wrote a newsletter informing them of what was going on at WRU and at home.

Fortunately, many of my friends who served returned to long and successful lives. Skippy Friedman, my fellow Kinsman Cowboy, had a tough go of it in the Army. He fought at the horrific Battle of the Bulge in late 1944, where he was captured and served in a POW camp until he was liberated by the U.S. Army in the last month of the war as it marched toward Berlin. His reward for courageous service to his country was an opportunity to come home and pursue a fulfilling career as an attorney in Cleveland. "Life has been good ever since," he recently told me. Elmer Paul served as president of ZBT before joining the fight in WWII. He taught me a great deal about how to run a fraternity, which came in handy when I replaced him as president. Upon his return to the States, he embarked on a fruitful investment brokerage career.

It was very odd to be without a uniform, since everywhere I looked people called to active duty wore them. I felt shamed by my lack of the real thing. To compensate while awaiting my call up, I volunteered almost every night at the Stage Door Canteen downtown to entertain the enlisted men by singing and doing choral numbers with other students. In 1943, my call finally came when I received a dispatch from Major General Fred C. Wallace, stationed at an Army camp in Fort Hayes, near Columbus, Ohio.

Then a twist of fate, so to speak, later kept me from the war. In the spring of 1943, the college staged a fraternity track meet. All of the members of ZBT who hadn't gone to training camps or shipped out were asked to participate. Elmer, our president, asked me to represent us in the high jump event, even though I had never in my life even attempted a high jump. No one else had volunteered for that event. I loved my fraternity and wanted to help out in any way I could, especially since we were short-handed, so I accepted the challenge.

On the day of the event, I was a little nervous, but my fraternity brothers were very supportive, cheering and applauding as I ran toward the high jump bar and flung my body over it with my long legs following. Unfortunately, I hadn't had a lot of time to practice or develop good form. I managed to get my body slightly twisted in the air, which caused me to descend awkwardly and land hard on my left leg. I heard a crack as I hit the pads. I thought I had broken my leg. Instead, I had torn cartilage in my left knee. This injury was to have immediate consequences, and it bothered me for the rest of my life.

Soon after the intra-fraternity track meet, my father, at the age of 52, suffered a heart attack. Everything at Weiss Restaurant was going well, but he was probably working too much with too little rest. Each morning I drove to see my father at Lakeside Hospital (now part of University Hospitals Case Medical Center). The Western Reserve University (now Case Western Reserve University) campus has always been intertwined with University Hospitals' campus. Back then, Lakeside's parking lot was conveniently adjacent to both the ZBT house on Abington Road and my first class, so I walked through it all the time.

On April 8, 1943, one day before my 20th birthday, I followed my regular routine, heading to the hospital to visit my father before going to class. When I got near his room, I was turned away rather abruptly by an intern who led me to a waiting room at the end of the hall. I tried to shoot past him, but he grabbed my shoulders and ordered me not to go to the room. "You're father died during the night," he said. "He had another attack and we couldn't revive him. He is dead."

Walking out of the hospital, I knew I was in no condition to attend class. I drove home, dreading the thought of having to tell my mother. It was one of the hardest things I've ever had to do. She was terribly upset, almost inconsolable. We all cried for some time. I can't even remember how long we sat there in a daze.

Jack and I took it upon ourselves to support my mother emotionally and financially, as she struggled through this difficult time. Of course, in the midst of all of it, I received a dispatch from General Wallace ordering me into active duty. The timing couldn't have been worse. I decided to call Fort Hayes and asked to speak directly to General Wallace. You couldn't do that today, but back then, they put me right through to him. I informed the General of my father's recent death and that my mother needed me at her side, especially since Jack had to care for his own family. "You are now on a six-week furlough, Private Weiss," he ordered. I always admired his great compassion.

My mother was relieved when I told her his decision. Six weeks later, though, there I was reporting for duty. During my physical, the doctor carefully examined my recently injured left knee. Unsatisfied with the lingering damage to the cartilage, he said, "I am reclassifying you to 1-C because you can't march at all." This led to an A-6 honorable discharge.

On one hand, I was relieved, knowing that I could help my mother. On the other hand, I felt tremendous guilt over not serving, since so many of my friends were fighting all over the world to keep us free. Sheila kids me that I was just jealous because I couldn't walk around wearing a uniform. I mean, you're talking about a tall, slender guy who later, as a professional, loved to wear fine dress clothes so much that some people even called me "The Suit." But that wasn't it. I wanted to be in the trenches next to my friends and fraternity brothers.

With my plans for a heroic military career dashed, I turned my attentions to landing a full-time job and a steady income to contribute on the home front. Since I didn't have a lot of practical experience to offer, I came up with the idea to write an off-the-wall letter of introduction that would catch people's eye. I took a bit of a risk and forsook the standard, dry business document and crafted a letter laced with creativity, personality and humor. I didn't know how to type, and there were no copy machines then, so I enlisted my girlfriend, Ruth Abelson, to pound out nine copies of the letter with the names and addresses of the presidents of the top nine advertising agencies in Cleveland and Akron. Of the seven responses I received, two contained requests for job interviews.

One of them came from Allen Billingsly, the president of Fuller, Smith & Ross, Cleveland's largest ad agency in the 1940s. My job title? Legman. I became the Federal Express of the day, as I was responsible for carrying print ad layouts and copy back and forth from the agency to Westinghouse Appliance, our rather sizable client in Mansfield, Ohio, about 80 miles southwest of Cleveland. I liked my new field, and I was eager to learn as much as possible. Bernice Fluke and Olive Gately, two amazing women who wrote the ads, taught me a lot. But my first true indoctrination into the wacky world of advertising came from Stanley Patno, the senior account manager that I reported to directly every day.

In 1945, as the grim war operations in Europe and the Pacific lurched to their conclusions, John Mitcheltree, an account manager of FSR, frequently counseled me about potential career options. One day, though, he advised me to go back to college. "You are a Dartmouth Man, Marc," he declared. "I want to introduce you to my friend, Red Flynn, who is in charge of recruitment for Dartmouth College and lives in Cleveland."

By then, I was pretty happy where I was. I finally felt that I was on track for a career in advertising. I no longer held any aspirations to complete my college education that had been so rudely interrupted by world war and my father's death. I certainly had no hope of attending an Ivy League institution. After all, three years earlier, Harvard had rejected my application, so you can imagine my surprise and joy when I was accepted to Dartmouth.

I spent the next few months planning my move to New England. I saved as much money as I could. I said my good-byes and shared as much time with my mother as possible. She was excited about this opportunity for me, and I knew she would miss me. We had grown quite close over the past couple of years, but she was doing much better now and Jack was there to help her, so I knew I could leave. I packed my beat-up old suitcase, and on a sunny morning in August, I caught a bus to the train station downtown, bought my ticket, and then jumped on the train to my first destination outside of Cleveland: Hanover, New Hampshire.

I immediately fell in love with the campus and the New England terrain. Growing up in Cleveland, I was used to the cold and snow, though I never did learn how to ski in the surrounding mountains. I started to figure out that someone up there wanted me to have strong writing skills, as I had two incredible instructors. In a creative writing course, Professor Stearns Morse taught us about the writing craft and all its intricate details and nuances. My classmates possessed a tremendous amount of writing talent, too. Just like at WRU, several remained friends for many years. One long-time pal who sat next to me in class was Lowell Thomas, Jr., the son of the famous world-traveler and news anchor. The professor gave A's to everyone in the class. No one complained or asked for a reevaluation.

The poet-in-residence that year was Robert Frost, who by then had become the quintessential New Englander, formal and straightforward but with a delightfully wry sense of humor. He was always very nice to me and the other students. Frost had actually attended Dartmouth in 1892 for less than a semester, before taking a break to teach and write, enrolling at Harvard several years later. We would sit at a table or on the floor around him, and we would all read what we had written and then discuss our poetry or short stories. Frost would talk to us about our writing. Sometimes, he would read his poetry to us at the end of class or give readings in the library. His reading and interpretation of his own poetry taught me about the beauty of simple, crisp phrasing and words that bring pictures to the mind. That was one of the best and most memorable parts of my college education.

I had been granted a full scholarship for tuition, but I needed a job to help pay my expenses. My first position at a bowling alley was a, well, uncomfortable one. They had all 6'2" of me cramped behind the alley, setting pins, because at that time, they weren't automatic. You had to hand-set them. I jumped a million miles high the first time a ball slammed into the rack of pins right in front of me, sending them flying in all directions. I made it through the day, but then I went to the boss and said, "This just isn't for a Jewish boy, sir. I could get killed by those bowling pins."

My next employment was much calmer. I got a job in the kitchen at the Hanover Inn restaurant. I made salads. The chef was very nice to me and fed me steak or roast beef. As Sheila says, it was the perfect job for me. I love to eat. For my 60th birthday, we took Jennifer, our beautiful daughter, on a trip to Hanover and had dinner at the Inn. I informed the waitress that I had once made salads there. When she came back to the table, she told me, "The chef says he could use you tonight."

My favorite job while I was at Dartmouth, though, was my time working as sports editor for the weekly newspaper, *The Green Light*. My roommate,

Richard Hyman, played right field for Dartmouth's team, so I watched a lot of baseball games. I had a particularly interesting experience covering a Dartmouth-Yale game one day, though I wasn't to know exactly how interesting until many years later. I was so intrigued by the play of Yale's first baseman, a tall, rangy kid who was a fluid fielder, that I decided to interview him after the game so I could write a column about him. I introduced myself, and he shook my hand and said his name was George Bush. I had no idea at the time I was watching the future 41$^{st}$ President of the United States playing baseball.

I also sang in the men's glee club. We traveled all around New England, performing at different schools, churches and nursing homes. I enjoyed singing anytime I had an opportunity.

I loved Dartmouth and treasure my experiences there to this day. But once again, a number of divergent influences converged to change my life, and in this case, bring me home. Before I left Cleveland, I had gotten into a pretty serious relationship with Lois Wohlgemuth. Lois worked as a feature reporter for the *Cleveland Press* and as Cleveland correspondent for *Life Magazine*. When *Life* gave her assignments, they would send a photographer from New York to cover the story, including, on occasion, Alfred Eisenstaedt, who had already established himself as an exceptional photojournalist. Eisenstaedt and Lois hit it off, and he even became good friends with my brother Jack.

Unbeknownst to me, my loved ones in Cleveland were taking action to bring me back to my hometown. Lois and Jack each approached Dean Huntley of Western Reserve University and asked him to accept all my Dartmouth credits. Once he agreed, their argument was that, if I transferred back to WRU, I could complete my degree in less than a year. Lois wanted to get married, and Jack, who was already married and had four young children, realized he needed help caring for our widowed mother. I wrestled with the decision, because things were going so well at Dartmouth, but they finally convinced me. I guess the prospect of mom's home cooking combined with other obvious advantages provided an inducement. So, I returned to Cleveland. I graduated from Western Reserve University in June 1946 with a Bachelor of Arts degree in English, one year sooner than if I had remained at Dartmouth.

That fall, I found a job as advertising manager for a half-size (a euphemism for plus-size women) dress company. I was employed and learning, but I was becoming increasingly restless and bored. More than anything now, I wanted to start my own business. I knew persistence would pay off. So, I constantly devised and developed new ideas. The underlying goal was to combine my brief but diverse experience to that point with my writing skills, innate leadership capabilities and growing business acumen. Finally, I set aside a number of business ideas that I had brainstormed, scribbled down and grappled with every day and sometimes late into the night to pursue one: a trade magazine called *Counterpoints* that would target department store salespeople and their customers at the point of sale.

*Counterpoints* would provide department store sales trainers with all of the information they needed to make their sales staff more effective at selling specific products. For example, our articles would explain advantageous product features and list all the reasons why a customer would want to purchase those items. Before I could launch the publication, though, I had to overcome one major challenge: finding a way to convince the training directors to pay for shipments of the magazines so they could give them to their sales force. First, I had to visit all of the stores to sell the training directors on making that commitment; then I had to convince the various product manufacturers to advertise in *Counterpoints*. No easy task, especially since I was still working and had to do it all on my own time.

With the enthusiastic support of Lois and Jack, who had a business degree and was moving up the ranks at a Cleveland publishing firm, I contacted a reputable attorney, Henry Gottfried. I gave him a detailed presentation about my concept. He and Jack both encouraged me to call Jack's boss,

Irving Hexter, president of Industrial Publishing Company, who owned a number of trade magazines. I gave him my little dog-and-pony show, including a copy of the rough dummy layout. He was interested, he said, but hesitant because two years before, a similar publication he tried to launch had failed. The success of our magazine, I argued, would arise from his guidance and the wisdom he had acquired from that very experience.

Still, he needed time to consider our idea thoroughly. I was anxious, so I returned to Mr. Gottfried to explore with him any other options for investors should Mr. Hexter turn us down. As we reviewed the concept once more, he decided right there that he would finance the project himself. Part of our deal included start-up office space in one of his spare offices. He also introduced me to a friend of his who owned a printing company and offered us a decent price.

Both of those contributions gave us a little traction, but we had many greater issues to address. He assumed that, as an ambitious, bright young man, I could handle all of the challenges and produce immediate results. The problem was neither one of us knew enough about publishing a magazine to anticipate all of the vital concerns.

After my second meeting with Mr. Gottfried, I returned home with the happy news and asked Lois to serve as editor of *Counterpoints*. She had proven herself a talented writer and quick, creative thinker, and she immediately suggested several good ideas. We invited monthly columns by *Esquire Magazine* on menswear, *Harper's Bazaar* for women's fashions, and *Good Housekeeping* on how to successfully sell appliances to consumers. Each accepted our request.

Drawing on my bent for sales, I focused on building circulation for *Counterpoints*. I recorded several early successes. Higbee's was the first Cleveland department store to sign up. Shortly afterward, Marshall Fields in Chicago and Bullocks in Los Angeles came onboard. That was the easy part. We hit a genuine business landmine in trying to sell fashion professionals on the idea. They weren't interested in our broad coverage of just about every type of product sold in a department store, including home appliances. That revealed our mistake: We overreached. Instead of being highly focused, our publication addressed numerous diverse audiences, not pleasing any one.

If that weren't bad enough, in our ignorance of the industry, Mr. Gottfried and I had woefully miscalculated, and our financial projections for start-up costs ended up falling far short of reality. To achieve the level of sales that we needed, we would have to spend a lot more than we had estimated to cover office set-up, travel, photography and circulation. The bills continued to pile up, and to be honest, I ran out of energy. I was doing the work of ten people and running in multiple directions.

The decision to close down was easy. We just couldn't afford to waste any more money. Ultimately, painfully, we learned a great deal. We didn't know it then, of course, but those hard-earned lessons would benefit us in the years to come. Fortunately, neither of us had abandoned our day jobs. In 1947, Lois and I got married and moved in with her family in University Heights.

Although I was deeply frustrated and anxious in the wake of our false start with *Counterpoints*, I was still confident that I was destined to be a self-made man. Entrepreneurism ran in my blood. My father's father, Isaac Angelovich (1845-1935), was a successful businessman in Gernyes, Hungary, where he owned thousands of acres of property and ran a popular general store, tavern and horse livery. We affectionately refer to his business as Avis Rent-a-Horse. We even keep a sizable model of a general store and a man on horseback in our kitchen as a tribute to my industrious grandfather.

My father and mother went on to own and operate Weiss Restaurant, which my mother continued to run with my uncle after my father's death.

Jack worked as an editor at the Industrial Publishing Company and then struck out on his own to become publisher of *Properties Magazine* for the rest of his professional career.

Now, as the 1940s came to a close, like my grandfather, father, mother and brother before me, I knew in my heart and in my head that it was time to launch my own business. I didn't have to wait long.

# 3 | Wyse in Business

In 1951, I was 29 years old, ambitious, desirous of running my own company, with a mixed résumé and one failure as a magazine publishing magnate at 25. Still, the more I looked at our assets, the more I knew our concept for a new business was correct: Find an effective way to combine my sales ability with Lois's writing skills. We just had to refine it.

One day I was thinking about the success Nancy Sasser had had with her advertising column in national magazines. Why couldn't we do that? Lois could write better than Nancy, and I knew I could sell. I called on Grant Stone, the business manager of the now-defunct *Cleveland Press*, to pitch my idea for an editorialized ad column for shoppers. We met in his office, where I proudly rolled out the dummy layout for "Wise Buys by Lois." He turned me down flat. He said it would interfere with his local sales department.

Convinced that persistence pays, I met with Leo Doyle, Grant's counterpart at the *Cleveland News*, the afternoon newspaper rival of the *Press*. Doyle liked "Wise Buys" immediately. He even gave me free access to a cartoonist in their advertising department so we could perk up our two- or three-inch columns with a small illustration for each advertiser. We charged $19.04 a week for a two-inch column and $28.56 for a three-inch column. Doesn't seem like much today, but these were 1951 prices, and we included a nice mark-up. Initially, we did most of our "Wise Buys" sales and writing on Saturdays or during lunch hours. To pay our bills, I continued to labor in my advertising manager position at the half-size dress company, and Lois wrote movie reviews and feature stories for the *Cleveland Press*.

All of our early advertisers — including a laundry, optical store, camera retailer, pharmacy, carpeting store and the East Ohio Gas Company — signed 13-week contracts. At last, we were on our way. Eventually, the *Cleveland News* was bought by Cleveland's morning newspaper, *The Plain Dealer*, so "Wise Buys" now appeared and flourished in a more far-reaching retail environment. We ran two full columns twice a week. Our burgeoning little business provided us enough income to not only quit our jobs, but put down a deposit on a new house in University Heights.

While our house was being built, we lived in a tiny apartment near charming Shaker Square. Located in Cleveland proper, the Square borders Shaker Heights, a fairly affluent suburb which at the time boasted the country's highest per capita income, according to the U.S. Census Bureau. Built in the 1920s by the Van Sweringen brothers around the same time they were building the Terminal Tower downtown and the Shaker Rapid Transit line that connects the two, the country's second planned residential shopping center is distinguished by its attractive architecture. Before the shopping mall phenomenon hit in the 1970s, the Square drew numerous upper-income visitors from the Cleveland suburbs to shop at tony boutiques or patronize several restaurants. Although it has changed a lot over the years, it remains a vibrant historic district.

Getting back to 1951, though, Lois and I often had dinner at the busy and beautiful Stouffer Restaurant at the Square that had opened shortly after World War II. Unbeknownst to us, our choice of fine dining establishments was about to turn into our first big break.

The manager of Stouffer's was a friendly man named Wally Blankenship. Ambitious and enterprising, he always looked for new ways to attract customers. He could hardly serve more guests, because the restaurant was packed every day for lunch and dinner. At a time when the word "innovation" wasn't batted around as much as it is now, Wally responded to his customers' frequent requests for take-home meals they could reheat and serve. He figured he could drive profits by freezing some of the restaurant's favorite menu items and offering them for sale in a freezer cabinet next to the cashier's counter. The biggest seller was Stouffer's macaroni and cheese, which Wally packaged in an aluminum dish wrapped in a light blue package. It sold for 39 cents or 3 for $1.00. Nobody prepared better frozen-food dishes than Stouffer's. Not then. Not today.

We knew right away that it was the perfect item for our column. Wally bought a three-inch ad in "Wise Buys," and it worked! Soon he and his boss, Vernon Stouffer, realized they had the beginnings of promising new business, Stouffer's Frozen Foods. Little did they know how huge a business it would become. They certainly never imagined it would one day dwarf their six-city restaurant chain and become America's premier frozen food line, offering more than 150 varieties of prepared foods. That's a big jump from the handful of delicacies available in Wally's freezer.

Stouffer Restaurants in Cleveland, Pittsburgh and Detroit started carrying their frozen-food packages, and business was brisk. Stouffer favorites such as spinach soufflé, escalloped apples, tuna noodle casserole and Vernon's favorite, Lobster Newburg, soon joined "mac and cheese" in the freezer cabinets. Pleased with the enthusiastic response, Stouffer Foods continued to expand its advertising in "Wise Buys." Wally hired a bright, young sales manager named Phil Fields. Phil liked "Wise Buys," but he wanted more. "Can't you do radio or regular newspaper ads or even table tents for the restaurant?" he asked. "Sure," we said. Wyse Advertising was now officially in business.

All of a sudden, we were an advertising agency with our first client, Stouffer's Frozen Foods. Instead of cranking out a lot of ads, though, we designed eye-catching signs and table tents for their restaurants that reminded customers to take home their favorite Stouffer frozen foods. Vernon was nervous about spending money for advertising. After all, it was still a small business.

Phil, however, started selling to food brokers in Cleveland, Pittsburgh and Detroit, and they, in turn, sought distribution in food stores and large supermarkets. Advertising and point-of-sale branding became essential, so we added local radio. I remember going to Pittsburgh and sitting in my hotel room all day listening to the radio to make sure our Stouffer spots were running. It was the only way we could be sure back then.

At that time, who would have dreamed that Stouffer's would become the giant in the frozen food industry? We spent hours and hours in agonizing discussions and tasting sessions trying to determine what items to freeze. Talk was plentiful. Advertising money was scarce. Plans were submitted and approved, but often cancelled at the last minute by a nervous Vernon Stouffer. He was a great restaurant man, not a great marketer. Phil Fields wanted a pizza in the line or at least lasagna. Vernon was horrified because Italian dishes were never on Stouffer Restaurant menus. He championed the Lobster Newburg. In frustration, Phil left the company. He was ultimately replaced by a brilliant businessman named Bill Lassiter. Lassiter was fresh out of Cresap, McCormick and Paget, one of the country's top consulting companies in New York. He brought sophisticated thinking, planning and marketing to the company. He saw Stouffer's one day being a $100 million or more enterprise. His projections proved correct, as today Stouffer's sales figures keep the company locked in the "largest brand in the freezer case" position.

Because Stouffer's frozen foods evolved from their restaurant, they had introduced a premium, high-end segment to the frozen food market with a focus on packaging single entrées loaded with meat and vegetables, rather than the whole meals or "TV dinners" that C.A. Swanson & Sons sold in supermarkets in the mid-'50s. With their emphasis on quality over mass production, Stouffer's volume of frozen food business grew so robustly that, in 1954, the company purchased a small factory on Woodland Avenue next to a farmer's market in Cleveland's inner city to serve as a pilot processing plant. Two years later, the company was officially named Stouffer Foods Corporation. Vernon promoted Wally and put his ex-restaurant manager in charge of their new frozen foods division. He picked the right man. Wally set up a frozen foods kitchen line and hired home economist Ruth Dengler and women cooks to prepare foods the Stouffer way: high-quality ingredients and home-style cooking.

Both Lois and I learned a lot from Bill Lassiter. He taught us how to think critically and strategically about advertising. He organized Stouffer's resources and ran roughshod over anyone who couldn't keep up. As a result, he wasn't very popular with some of the management team. We were crazy about him, though, because he made Stouffer's a strong, stable business. Unfortunately, the rapid growth of the company worked against us. One day while Vernon was having lunch at The Union Club, Cleveland's prestigious city club where business and civic leaders make big plans, his friends asked him who his advertising agency was. When he said, "Wyse Advertising," they said, "Who? You should talk to J. Walter Thompson, the big advertising guns in New York."

First thing the next day, seven suits from J. Walter showed up at Vernon's office. Vernon hired them, and we and our young agency were out. We were crushed. With Lassiter's guidance, we had started running effective television and print ads in several markets. Good things were starting to happen. Lassiter was told that he now had to work with J. Walter Thompson to promote frozen foods. There was nothing he could do about it, but he persuaded Vernon to keep us as the agency for Stouffer Restaurants. Years later, that would lead to the substantial Stouffer Hotel account, which eventually became larger than the frozen food division by the time it was sold to a Hong Kong-based hotel chain for a reported $1.5 billion in 1993.

Vernon had promised Lassiter that he would make him president of the entire Stouffer Corporation. When that didn't happen, Lassiter left Stouffer's. Lois and I were sad to see him leave, since he had mentored us as we launched our fledgling ad agency and drove us to always pursue exceptional, productive campaigns for our clients. Truly, he set us on a long-term path of success. Vernon saw Lassiter's exit as an opportunity to bring in his son-in-law,

Jim Biggar, to run the marketing of the frozen food company. Jim seemed unsuited for the job because he came from Reliance Electric, an industrial company that manufactured motors — a far cry from the frozen food business. Worse still, he was Vernon's son-in-law.

Jim Biggar turned out to be the greatest surprise of all. He was an astute marketer, thinker and planner. Intensely dedicated to quality, he was a considerate business leader and well-suited to growing the business. I quickly realized he was the right choice because he understood how important the quality of Stouffer's Foods was to shoppers and to future success. He built a bright young team of sales and marketing people. Don Stover headed up sales and hired an aggressive group of food brokers. Bob McQuiggin was a brilliant marketing man who knew how to position the line and price each product. In the 1980s, he introduced the fabulously successful "Lean Cuisine" line for health-conscious customers. Alan McDonald, a former Stouffer Restaurant manager, became president of the frozen foods company when Vernon elevated Biggar to chairman of the board. The business was flourishing, but suddenly things started to go awry when Vernon faced a major and very delicate decision.

Vernon's son Jim had joined the restaurant part of the business and was beginning to voice strong opinions, while his son-in-law Jim Biggar was suddenly outperforming the restaurants. Vernon's dilemma: Who would succeed him at the helm, Jim S. or Jim B.? To complicate matters, his business attention waned once he became the new owner of the Cleveland Indians baseball team in 1966. A fateful and disastrous move. He didn't know a ball from a strike or how expensive running a ball club could be. Alvin Dark was his manager, and the darkest days were ahead for the hapless Indians.

Beleaguered by baseball reverses and agonizing family loyalties, Vernon made what turned out to be his worst decision of his life. In 1967, he sold the company to Litton Industries, a large West Coast company then headed by "whiz kids" Tex Thornton and Roy Ash, who, among other advanced electronics, had pioneered the development of the commercial microwave oven, so it seemed like a glamorous move. Litton was a red-hot conglomerate at a time when Wall Street was interested in the big build-up deal. There seemed to be an obvious synergy, too. Litton owned a microwave oven company, and Stouffer's made these delicious frozen foods that could be quickly heated in the microwaves. What a natural combination. Vernon got Litton stock for his company. It was selling for more than $100 per share. Vernon was off the family hook. Let Litton decide his successor; Vernon's investments would be well-cared for by his huge bundle of Litton stock certificates.

How wrong could he be? Wall Street soon soured on conglomerates and especially Litton, which was all over the lot. Hardly any synergy existed between microwave ovens and Stouffer Frozen Foods, because they were both sold at different kinds of outlets. Litton stock plummeted into the low teens, and the banks and Vernon Stouffer became very nervous. The ownership title to the Cleveland Indians lay in the National City Bank vault. Because Vernon had the respect of the entire business community, the banks delayed foreclosure proceedings. It came very close, though, until Vernon found another buyer, a group led by Cleveland Cavaliers and Cleveland Barons owner Nick Mileti, in 1972. One of the interested groups was headed by George Steinbrenner, who then bought the New York Yankees in 1973.

Litton tapped Bob Bruder, who had directed their microwave oven business in America, to run Stouffer's. After all, he had introduced Vernon to Thornton and Ash. Not much of a qualification, but he had earned a finder's reward. Wyse Advertising was by now a growing agency, and Bruder and his Litton Industries microwave ovens was a client with big potential. We knew Bruder. He had been a client for more than a year, and we were sure he was in way over his head. Bruder was a classic egomaniac: nervous, fidgety, and incessantly talking about himself. His relationship with all the Stouffer people was chaotic at best, especially with those who had been key members of Lassiter's team. As the Litton stock tumbled, he and Vernon Stouffer actually traded punches at Cleveland's bastion of gentlemanly behavior, The Union Club. Under Litton and Bruder, Stouffer Restaurants deteriorated rapidly. Many of the well-trained managers, cooks, and bartenders left, as they were instructed to follow dubious new rules and regulations. For example, as a cost-savings measure, the amount of alcohol poured in a martini or Manhattan had been cut in half, which cut the customer count by almost as much.

Nevertheless, as the Stouffer Restaurants sagged, the Frozen Foods Division, under Jim Biggar's guidance, continued to grow and prosper. He made sure their products that were now distributed in supermarkets across the United States maintained their quality. Thornton and Ash gave Biggar free reign, as he was building a productive and profitable asset for Litton. Knowing the Whiz Kids were not only adept at acquiring, but were sellers, too, Biggar set up a plan to re-acquire the company. He told Thornton of his mission and carefully assembled a group of well-heeled Cleveland investors, banks, and Stouffer Frozen Food executives who were eager to buy the company. Everyone was set to do the deal. Except for one key player, Tex Thornton.

One Friday afternoon in 1973, the telephone rang in Biggar's office. It was Thornton on the line. "Jim, meet me at the Regency Hotel in New York on Monday at 10:00 am," he said.

"Great," Biggar responded, elated at the prospect of closing the deal on Monday. "I'll be there."

Monday morning, his airplane arrived at LaGuardia on time. He urged the cab driver to be aggressive in the early traffic, and precisely at ten o'clock, he knocked on the door of Thornton's Regency Hotel suite. Thornton greeted him. There were three or four men sitting on couches and chairs behind him.

"Jim, I want you to meet Pierre Liotard-Vogt," Thornton said. "He is the managing director of Nestlé, and he has just bought your company."

Biggar was stunned. Not normally a man who spoke profanities, he heard one come out of his angry mouth. For a moment, he leered defiantly at Thornton, refused to shake anybody's hand and walked out of the suite. When the news reached the other key Stouffer executives in Cleveland, the response was rebellion. However, Liotard-Vogt had given Thornton a check for $100 million, and he knew exactly how to handle this situation. Nestlé, S.A. (Switzerland) was accustomed to operating as a non-resident owner. Less than 5 percent of Nestlé's multibillion-dollar sales are done in its home country. Today, it is the world's largest food company, with sales of more than $100 billion. Liotard-Vogt arrived in Cleveland a few days later with hat in hand. He even insisted on carrying his own luggage from the airport taxi to the Stouffer offices on PlayhouseSquare. He bore the demeanor of a humble man. He met with Biggar, McDonald, McQuiggin, and Stover and promised them full autonomy to run the business. He promised them all the financial support they needed to achieve the potential they knew existed. He promised them substantial bonus opportunities. They finally accepted his proposals. With that, the $100 million price tag turned out to be one of the biggest bargains ever recorded in the food industry.

Biggar now had the plants and the marketing monies to dominate the frozen prepared foods industry. Stouffer's French pizza, lasagna, spaghetti and meatballs, as well as the fabulously successful Stouffer's Lean Cuisine products all found their way to America's dinner tables. The prices were a little high and the calories and sodium content were somewhat out of hand, but for several incredible years, the frozen food division was unchallenged. Parent company Nestlé reaped huge profits, while Biggar and his team stood as the big American heroes in Vevy, Switzerland. So much so that, in 1991, Biggar was named to head up Nestlé companies in the United States, from the candy companies, beverages, vegetable packing, and baby foods to the chain of hotels.

In 1951, that titanic success for Jim and Stouffer's was still decades away. Wyse Advertising was a two-person firm with one account and a long way to go. But I finally had my own business. Not a bad way to start, either.

# 4 | A Little Luck Never Hurts

In the early years at our advertising agency, we were fortunate to have an ootzer. Everybody needs an ootzer in his life. Who's an "ootzer"? Sometimes it's your wife. Sometimes it's your mother-in-law. What's an "ootzer"? An ootzer is a non-stop talker, an incessant nag. He calls you in the middle of the day or late at night and whispers to you on the phone. He's on you to make that call, to write that letter. An ootzer reminds you of your pending obligations time and again. Finally, to keep an ootzer quiet, you do what he tells you to do.

The ootzer in my life was a guy named Pete Hlinka. He was the sales manager for WEWS Channel 5, the ABC affiliate network in Cleveland. To him I owe a great deal. It was at his insistence that I made a phone call to schedule a meeting with Jesse Grover Bell, the founder and president of Bonne Bell Cosmetics. J.G., as he was best known, had launched the company in 1927 from his basement in Salina, Kansas, where he made his early skin care concoctions on a hot plate and then sold them door-to-door. His wife, Mame, loved them because they cleared her skin. He named the company for his lovely daughter. In 1916, before she was born, he had read in the *Saturday Evening Post* a serialization of Emerson Hough's novel, *The Man Next Door*, in which the heroine is named Bonne Bell. He and Mame liked the story and the character so much they chose that name for their second baby girl.

Anyway, back then, Pete's station carried "The Paige Palmer Show," which was the precursor to Jazzercise®, as Palmer had produced the first televised fitness and exercise program for women in the U.S. that had debuted in 1948. Palmer was an attractive blonde with a boyish bob, and her show had numerous female viewers nationwide who, Pete pointed out, represented potential purchasers of Bonne Bell cosmetic products.

So, at my ootzer's insistence, I called J.G. He sounded like a very happy man, with a deep, gravelly voice and a wild, loud laugh. The next morning, Lois and I drove to Lakewood, a suburb on the West Side of Cleveland, where Bonne Bell had its headquarters in a beautiful, Georgetown-style building they had completely and lavishly refurbished. University Heights, where we were living then, is on the East Side. We arrived ten minutes early for an 8 a.m. appointment, and we were surprised to be ushered into J.G.'s third-floor office immediately. He was seated at his desk, clutching the phone to his ear and conversing loudly into the mouthpiece. He fit the person I imagined when I spoke to him on the phone: a big, gregarious man with a broad smile and a hearty laugh that shook the whole office. We sat in two chairs facing his desk and waited. He was selling the person on the other end on what by that time had become Bonne Bell's best-known product, a camphor astringent called 10-0-6 lotion. Originally, it had been formulated to provide a general-purpose skin cleaner and freshener for women, but it had also achieved popularity as an acne treatment for teenage girls.

Finally, he hung up the phone. "Now, what do you want?" he said.

"We're sorry to disturb you," I said.

"Not at all. That was the buyer from Lazarus," he replied. "He's a good friend of mine, so I had to take the call. We're doing great, by the way. I just talked to J.L. Hudson in Detroit, too." He was beaming with enthusiasm. "Now, what can I do for you?"

"Well, this is my wife, Lois," I continued. "We're starting an advertising agency, and we wanted to talk to you about your business." Having come from the dress industry, I knew about buyers and department stores, so I talked about my experiences in that realm for several minutes. We also showed him a feature story Lois had written for *The Cleveland Press* about an indelible lipstick called "Princess Pat." After the story ran, Higbee's Department Store sold all of its "Princess Pat" lipsticks.

"I don't have an agency at present," J.G. said.

"I thought you did. What happened?" I inquired.

"Well, last night some people from our agency came in for a meeting, and they were drunk," he revealed. "So, I fired them." With that, he pointed his finger at us and declared, "You are my new advertising agency."

We were stunned. This declaration came only fifteen minutes after we had met J.G. We had just come there to get acquainted. We hadn't even asked for his account, but there it was. I said, "But, Mr. Bell, we just met you. We hardly told you anything about ourselves. How can you hire us?"

He said, "Listen, the last thing my agency did was junk anyway. I need an agency, and you're it."

I said, "This is an easy business." Sometimes in business you just need a little luck. Later we learned to love J.G. and understand his impulsive style. We also loved the entire Bell family. That day, less than an hour after we got there, he introduced us to his sales manager, Bob Mittendorf, as Bonne Bell's new ad agency.

In our next meeting three days later, J.G. again did almost all of the talking. He kept telling us about all of the wonderful attributes of his miracle product, 10-0-6 lotion. He sounded like an old-time medicine man. This miracle lotion, he said, works as a skin cleanser, burn soother, antiseptic dandruff killer, wart healer, pimple chaser –

"Wait, hold on, Mr. Bell," I said. "Nobody will ever believe that." We didn't. I don't know if he even heard me; he just kept on talking. His blue eyes sparkled. His large, ruddy face was on fire, and he alternately laughed and coughed in huge torrents. His whole body seemed ignited for action, and I can truly say he was larger than life and quite possibly the most interesting man I ever met. As he continued his pitch, his boxy paws practically obscured the 10-0-6 and the Plus 30 Face Cream bottles as he passed them to us for inspection. This tough, farm-bred Kansan seemed too out of place with these delicate products for women, but we got used to that. J.G. could sell anything to anyone.

We started to learn more about this thriving company and the man who started it. In 1890, in tiny Salina, Kansas, he was born to be a salesman. Starting with nothing more than a suitcase filled with a couple dozen hand-filled bottles, a smile, the dogged spirit and drive of a man who had to succeed to feed his family, he sold his products door to door. Thirty-seven years later, after moving his company to Cleveland, he found a remarkable product that changed everything. In 1936, J.G. Bell purchased the formula for what became known as 10-0-6 from a Cleveland research chemist who had compounded it for a dermatologist. It was a golden liquid antiseptic skin cleanser and toner that was recommended for a multitude of skin problems. J.G. named it Bonne Bell 10-0-6, and the company developed new formulas specifically for oily or sensitive skin. In 1998, Bonne Bell actually discontinued their key product, but later relaunched it as Ten-O-Six, as they continued to expand their full-range line of cosmetics. Actually, J.G. was one of the first to recognize the potential for youth cosmetics and directed his company into those products long before others pursued the powerful market segment that became known as "teenagers." *Seventeen* formally identified this new group as consumers of tomorrow with disposable income today in 1944, near the end of World War II, when the magazine was founded.

I once asked J.G. why he chose Cleveland. As a salesman in Kansas, he noted in awe that most national sales contests he entered were won by people from Cleveland. I found out later that he had also seen a Cleveland bank ad touting the fact that roughly half of all Americans lived within a 500-mile radius of the city, which represented a potentially vast market for his products. In 1927, he decided to move his wife and three children and his new Bonne Bell business to Cleveland. It turned out to be a good decision. Sure, it was a struggle at first. He told us how he had rented a small office in an old building in downtown Cleveland. The rent was $10 a month, and he could only come up with the first month's rent. By the fourth month, the landlord was raising a real fuss. No rent. Our clever young entrepreneur grew pretty good at dodging the landlord, and he would come to his office to fill his bottles and pack his cases very early in the morning or late at night or on weekends. One Saturday afternoon, the landlord caught him. While he was coming down the freight elevator, the landlord cut off the power, and there he was stuck between the second and third floors. A mean-tempered man, the landlord yelled: "You'll rot in there, until you pay the rent!"

But J.G. was a tireless worker. He traveled the country all week and only came to his office on weekends to fill orders and get the mail. By the time we met this remarkable man, he had come a long way. His company was doing more than $2 million in sales annually, which was impressive in cosmetics. He continually improved his product and his packaging. He hired a chemist who developed new products. He got more doctors to approve the products. He bought machinery and set up a bottling line. He built a dedicated sales force for Bonne Bell, trained them and paid them well. If a buyer doubted the purity of 10-0-6 lotion, one of J.G.'s most messianic salesmen would actually drink the product in front of the bedazzled customer. It was a convincing demonstration. Immediately thereafter, his salesman would go to a hospital and have his stomach pumped. The lotion's main ingredient is isopropyl alcohol. This particular salesman, Bob Mittendorf, was from Akron. He eventually became J.G.'s sales manager, the man we met on our first day there.

One week after we had won, or I should say had been gifted, the Bonne Bell account, Lois and I went to the Concord Hotel in Kiamesha Lake, New York, for a long-planned vacation, the first since we'd been married. Yes, we were in the Borscht Belt — The Catskills. July that year, 1952, was an extremely hot one. One morning, as we sat at the pool in a stupor after having eaten one of the most magnificent breakfasts ever served by mankind, I was surprised to hear my name being paged on the loudspeaker. It was Larry Miller calling from Cleveland. He was our only employee. He did everything: answered the phone, typed letters, typed ad copy, wrote copy, kept the files straight, did layouts, made coffee — all for the staggering sum of $50 a week. Now, I could tell through the volume and tone of his voice that Larry was excited. "Marc," he shrieked, "J.G. just called. He wants to place an ad schedule in about twenty newspapers in Kansas."

"What ads?" I said. "We haven't done anything yet."

"He's sending me some ads that were done by his previous agency, and he wants to run them in Kansas."

"Why Kansas?"

"He's got relatives there, and he wants to show them how well he's doing."

"Makes sense."

"Marc, how do you run ads in Kansas?"

"I don't know," I said. "Call the Business Information Bureau at the Cleveland Public Library. They'll tell you how to do it." Larry called later to say he had placed ads in six Kansas towns. The billings amounted to $30,000, and we earned a 15 percent commission. When I got back to our lounge chairs at the pool, I smiled at my reclining wife and said, "While we've been lounging here at the pool, we made $4,500 in commission."

"Not a bad business," she said.

"Not bad at all," I said. "Pass the Coppertone."

When we got back, I met with J.G., and I said, "I see you on Paige Palmer. Are you planning to go national?"

He laughed that booming laugh of his and said, "Yeah, got any ideas?"

"Why, yes, I do," I responded. "I'll be back in a week to offer our strategy." We shook hands. When we met again, I told him that we believed teenagers were an ideal national target market, and the best way to reach them would be radio ads. "Radio? Why not TV?" he asked.

"Radio takes copy and puts pictures into people's minds," I explained. "TV has a tendency to make people watching ads get sleepy, and I want action on 10-0-6 lotion." After telling me he loved the way I talked, J.B. bellowed, "Let's go."

From a marketing standpoint, 10-0-6 lotion was an enigma. It had too many uses. We decided to focus on one: teenage skin problems. The lotion had significant growth potential, and teenagers could be reached easily and effectively. With radio as our preferred media choice, the market-by-market spokesmen were the disc jockeys who dominated the dials in their home cities. To help Bonne Bell publicize their lotion nationwide, I invented the 10-0-6 test, and then we promoted it across the U.S. Point-of-sale cards with pictures of the top local DJs were placed on department store and drug store cosmetic counters inviting people to take the 10-0-6 test. The cards said, "Wash your face with soap and water. Now saturate a cleanser pad with 10-0-6 and gently rub your face. Notice the dirt and residue left on them. Proof that 10-0-6 absolutely cleans your skin's deepest pores." It worked. Beautifully, so to speak.

DJs from Boston to San Francisco were pushing the product on their programs by taking the test themselves and proclaiming the results. 10-0-6 lotion worked, even on their grizzled mugs. Eventually, many department stores assigned a person in their beauty departments to administer the test to shoppers. On top of that, the living, breathing Bonne Bell proved to be a charming and beautiful spokesperson, and she conducted teenage beauty exhibits all over the country. Bonne Bell 10-0-6 lotion was hot, and J.G. was on fire.

"Let's buy Chicago," he said. "We're in Walgreens, Marshall Fields, and Carsons. Who's the top disc jockey in Chicago?"

I replied, "Howard Miller on WIND. But he's expensive."

The next day I was at WIND trying to negotiate a schedule on the Howard Miller show. Jerry Glynn was the sales rep, and Ben Gage was the sales manager. They offered two deals — Miller's daily drive time show, and his Sunday two-hour specials. They were salesmen, too. They said, "Take your pick." J.G arrived at the radio station an hour later. Glynn and Gage explained the two options. Each option cost a lot of money. "I'll take them both!" J.G. said. Glynn and Gage were dumbstruck. They later told me it was the biggest order they ever took.

When J.G. was on fire, nothing could stop him. He asked me to join him when he called on the cosmetics buyer at Walgreens in Chicago. I was elated because I was curious to see J.G.'s pitch. In the buyer's office, J.G. lifted his heavy briefcase and plopped it on top of the desk. He reached in and fiddled around. The buyer was expecting samples. Instead, J.G. let loose his trademark giant, hearty guffaw. He pulled out a huge, size-12 pair of worn loafers that he explained belonged to his son, Jess. The laugh was infectious. We all roared. The happy buyer was sold.

Every Friday our office received a check from Bonne Bell paying their account in full. J.G., remembering his early days, insisted that his brother,

T.S., the company treasurer, clear the payables every Friday. J.G. now enjoyed carefree weekends with his close family. Thanks to our earnings from the Bonne Bell account, we had the money to expand a little bit. I hired a salesman, and together we sold to every new shopping center built in Cleveland during that time. We did radio ads for the big kickoff parties at the new centers. Often, Bonne Bell herself would make an appearance, along with Lois and me. We loved talking with the customers, who were mostly teenage girls worried about their skin. Bob Mittendorf frequently joined us. A highly effective salesman, he was full of enthusiasm and having a great time while 10-0-6 lotion continued to surge as a hot seller in grocery, drug, and department stores.

Unfortunately, skyrockets sometimes end up taking a hard landing. I'm not a psychiatrist, although analyzing client personalities in the advertising business somewhat qualifies me. Still, J.G. was one of the most fascinating case studies I ever encountered. I'm not sure of the scientific or medical name for it, but today we'd probably say he was bipolar. At first, for about six months of the year, J.G. would be absolutely on fire. When he was up, he was creative, enthusiastic, inspiring, courageous, optimistic, and entrepreneurial. He'd be training sales girls, setting up demonstrations, promotions and advertising programs or running around with me to newspapers, television, and radio stations, with his fountain pen poised to sign contracts. "What can we buy?" he'd always ask. One Friday, I went to visit J.G. at his office in Lakewood. He was on four phone calls simultaneously, talking constantly. I couldn't get his attention, and you just didn't interrupt J.G. So, I left him a note telling him I would be with one of his salesmen in New York the following Monday. On Monday, I walked into the Gotham Hotel in New York, and there was J.G. Since Friday, he had seen customers in Chicago, Miami and Jacksonville. When he was afire, he had enormous energy and drive!

The problem was, just as suddenly, he would go into hibernation, and for the next six months he would tear apart almost everything he had built. He would cancel all commitments. He believed the company was going out of business. He would stay in bed for days. What could have become another Revlon or Estée Lauder instead remained a small family business.

Eventually, Jess A. Bell, J.G.'s son, took control of the business in 1959. In 1972, Jess, a good athlete, started running to help him overcome his alcoholism, and he ran between 30 and 50 miles a week well into his 60s. He positioned Ten-O-Six lotion as the "healthy skin" lotion and he did very well with it. However, despite Jess's efforts, Bonne Bell essentially became a one-product company. He did enjoy some success with a flavored lip gloss called "Lip Smackers," as preteens loved it. Bonne Bell products aren't sold in department stores anymore. Today, you can find Ten-O-Six and their lip gloss products on the Internet or in mass market outlets such as Walmart. The beautiful Lakewood office where we so easily landed our first official new account after opening as an agency is gone now. In 1976, Jess moved the headquarters further west to a large plant and warehouse facility on 18 acres in Westlake with a two-mile running track, tennis and volleyball courts, gymnasium, and exercise rooms to promote their "Be Fit, Look Good" philosophy.

J.G. died in 1970 at the age of 80. Still, I often wonder what he would do now to boost distribution. Especially if J.G. were on fire.

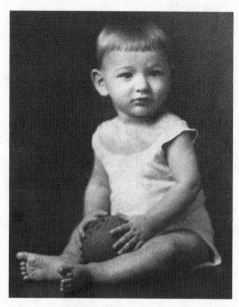

Demonstrating his preference for action early on, six-month-old Marc refused to sit still for the photographer until he gave him a ball, and then wouldn't stop fussing until he let him take it home.

The Kinsman Cowboy tosses a football with neighborhood friends near his family's home on East 154th Street.

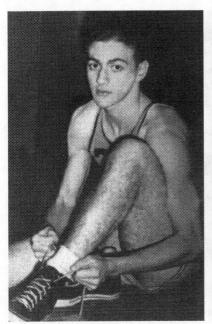

Marc laces up before a
varsity basketball game
his senior year (1940–41) at
John Adams High School.

At his full height of 6'2" by his senior
year at John Adams High School, Marc
shows off his agility under the hoop
and his belief that you won't make
a basket if you don't take a shot.

Marc sports his John Adams letter sweater while engaged
in another of his favorite activities: rehearsing a play.

Under Marc's (left) direction as Managing Editor his senior year, the John Adams High School *Journal* was named Best High School Newspaper in the U.S. by the National Scholastic Press Association.

Later known as "The Suit" for his sartorial splendor, Marc shows off his early dapper dressing skills in his John Adams graduation photograph.

Marc (center) exhibits his innate media acumen and love of radio as John Adams' Radio Bulletin Editor.

He may have left Cleveland briefly to attend Dartmouth College, but Marc took his love of sports and media with him, serving as Sports Editor for the school newspaper.

Marc assumes his Big Man on Campus pose in between classes at Western Reserve University (now Case Western Reserve University).

Marc and another college friend congratulate his old Kinsman chum Sydney "Skippy" Friedman's military uniform and status during World War II. Skippy was later captured at the Battle of the Bulge and ended the war as a POW, but made it home safely to a long career as a Cleveland attorney.

Marc, as always the tall one in the center, out on the town with a couple of sharp-dressed pals.

While on vacation in Florida in 1954, Marc stops on
the beach to admire his golden brown tan.

(L to R) Marc escorts his mother Jennie Wyse with his older
brother Jack in a photo taken on Mother's Day.

Destined to be together, Marc and Sheila could even turn a blind date into gold. Here they are 18 months later on their wedding day, May 22, 1983.

Dad with his darling daughter, Jennifer.

Marc's favorite photograph with Jennifer Wyse as a little girl, enjoying some peaceful beach time together.

In 2007, Sheila and Marc found just the right spot amongst the sun, sand, sea and palm trees to renew their wedding vows in Turks & Caicos.

The Wyses celebrate Marc's 80th birthday in 2003.

Marc with his good friend, the always vibrant
and entertaining Tommy Embrescia.

The Wyse Family in 2003: Back row left to right: Denise Wyse, Stephanie Wyse, Alex Wyse, Max Goldman, Kathy Wyse Goldman, Henry Goldman, Rob Wyse, Molly Goldman. Front row left to right: Jennifer Wyse, Emily Wyse, Marc & Sheila Wyse.

Marc in a reflective pose at his desk in his home
library where he wrote his memoirs.

# 5 | If You Don't Take the Shot, You Won't Make the Bucket

When I was playing basketball at Alexander Hamilton Junior High School, I learned a lifelong lesson. I was tall for my age and had played a lot of basketball as a kid, so I was ready for interscholastic play and quickly made the varsity squad. We were playing our archrival Nathan Hale Junior High at home in a very close and hard-fought contest. The gym was packed with anxious, cheering students, parents, and faculty.

As the final seconds of the game ticked down, I took possession of the ball. I raced up the court, and just past the half-court line, I realized I didn't have enough time to get to the key and attempt a layup or short jump shot. "Should I try from here?" I nervously thought. In the blink of an eye, I convinced myself that I should. I raised both arms, jumped as high as I could, and heaved the ball as hard as I could, arcing it toward the basket. The gym was almost completely silent, as if all the spectators were holding their breaths. As I watched my shot, the ball soared toward the ceiling, dropped toward the basket, and bounced off the backboard right through the hoop. The crowd erupted in cheers and screams, and the whole gymnasium seemed to shake with the surprise celebration. I'll never forget the wild uproar or the smell of bubblegum in the air that I'm pretty sure originated from our cute cheerleaders on the sidelines behind me.

That basket did two things: It won the game for us. And it crystallized a valuable lesson about risk that I have carried with me ever since that last-second victory and frequently applied throughout my business career: If you don't take the shot, you'll never make the basket.

I applied that lesson many times in our advertising business, the first time in 1952, not long after we landed the Bonne Bell account. Decades before the Foot Locker and Athlete's Foot stores were around, Higbee's opened a new sporting goods department in their downtown store. It was the twilight of the "Golden Age of Downtown Shopping," when Clevelanders still cherished the opportunity to travel downtown, walk up Euclid Avenue from Public Square to what is now known as PlayhouseSquare, and wander through the elegantly designed retail confines of Higbee's, Halle's, May Company, and Sterling Lindner-Davis. Founded as a dry goods shop in September of 1860, the Higbee Company had grown into a highly popular department store with annual sales around $40 million by the late '40s. Sales continued to increase into the '50s, but until the 1960s and '70s, Higbee's management refused to establish branch stores at the suburban shopping centers and malls that were sprouting everywhere.

Instead, they decided to renovate and add specialty sections for music and sporting goods, and expand their hospitality center on the 10$^{th}$ floor. Taking advantage of these urban retail attractions was easy for us, since Wyse Advertising now had an office downtown. So, as a neophyte golfer, I would peruse Higbee's sporting goods frequently to handle and feel all the golf clubs on display. That's how I got the inspiration for taking a shot: Why not sell Higbee's on television spots to promote its brand-new sporting goods department?

I called on Walter Powers, Higbee's ad manager. I was able to offer him a ten-second spot on the local NBC affiliate station in the National Open Golf Tournament. He bought it. The price was $200. I put a few picture slides of the department together with some descriptive copy and stayed home all Sunday afternoon to watch our first television commercial. Finally, Lou Worsham, the leader of the tournament appeared on the television screen. He had just hit his drive down the middle of the fairway, and he was

147 yards from the hole. He hit his approach shot, and the picture switched to a camera on the green watching his ball bouncing twice on the smooth green surface and then miraculously disappearing into the cup.

At that precise moment, the director at WNBK-TV in Cleveland cut from the startling Worsham eagle to the Higbee Sporting Goods spot. The next day, Higbee's telephones were jammed with calls from sports fans criticizing the store for interrupting the telecast at this history-making, memorable moment. Then it was my turn to receive a call. Walter Powers was livid with anger. "Well," I said, "it only proves that a lot of people saw your commercial."

Despite our initial bogey, my relationship with Higbee's began to flourish. The Higbee Music Center was the No.1 record store in town, and Bill Randle of WERE Radio was the No.1 disc jockey in town. I put them together. Randle was much more than a disc jockey. He was part of the music business. He had an incredible 60 percent share of the Cleveland radio audience. When he got behind a record, it was made. He knew the talent so well that the promoter and R&D men at the record companies would call to consult with him. Mitch Miller of CBS Records was a regular caller. Some of Randle's earlier discoveries were Johnny Ray, Guy Mitchell, Tony Bennett, Rosemary Clooney, The Four Lads, The Everly Brothers, and yes, Elvis Presley. On September 9, 1956, "The Pied Piper of Cleveland" introduced Elvis on his first appearance on "The Ed Sullivan Show," because Randle was supposedly the first radio personality to play an Elvis record outside of the South. In the 1950s, *Time* named him the top DJ in America.

Randle was very smart. He gained natural stature and so did his radio station. I would call Bill while he was on the air on WERE, Cleveland's leading station. Together, we would work out promotions for agency clients. He had a great deal of influence with recording companies and their star performers. He got Johnny Ray to come to the opening of the

Warren Village Shopping Center, an early Wyse client. We paid him the magnificent sum of $50. No wonder he sang his famous "Cry" ballad.

When Bill got behind a record, it became a hit. Cleveland became the bell cow for the record industry. One Sunday afternoon, Bill decided to feature a set of Glenn Miller albums. They were packaged together on 45-rpm discs. The price was $25 a set. Our client, the Higbee Music Center, set up operators to handle phone orders. That day they sold more than 1,100 albums — a total of $27,500 in retail sales, while the store was closed. People used their Higbee charge-a-plates. Another time Bill called excitedly and told me he could get Eddie Fisher to come to Higbee's and sign autographs. Eddie had just recorded "Oh, Mein Papa." He was the national teenage idol.

"Great," I said. "Let's do it."

Randle promoted it on the air for one day, and the next day at least 5,000 teenagers showed up on Higbee's main floor screaming for a view of little Eddie Fisher. They were shoving, and the noise was deafening. Suddenly, someone grabbed my shirt and tie. It was Ed Hoffman, the president of Higbee's.

"Get these kids outta here. They're gonna ruin our store," he yelled.

"Would you rather they go to the May Co. across the street?" I said. Hoffman released my shirt and walked away.

After the success with Higbee's Music Department, other buyers in the store were anxious to try radio to promote their departments. Dean Squires was the cosmetic buyer. He lined up co-op advertising funds from more than 25 cosmetic company suppliers, and we dominated the airwaves with a jingle that said, "Higbee's Cosmetic Department — The Secret of Cleveland's Most Beautiful Women." It was an enormous success, and

Dean left Higbee's to become president of a large cosmetics company in New York.

Later, the men's clothing buyer came to us to sell the Brandon Shop, his new section of bargain-priced suits. It was located on Higbee's Prospect Level. We had fun with that. And, "On the level! On the level! On Higbee's Prospect Level" became the vernacular in the city and answered consumers who might be skeptical of the low prices at the Brandon Shop.

The enormous consumer response and retail buzz was all very exciting to me. One day, I picked up a copy of *Broadcasting Magazine* and read that the Radio Advertising Bureau (RAB) in New York had offered to choose one department store in America for The $64,000 Challenge. The RAB represented almost every radio station in America. Its mission was to promote radio and its sales effectiveness. Of course, I already was convinced that most department stores at that time were wedded to old habits. That meant newspaper advertising.

So, I picked up the phone and called the RAB in New York. Their dynamic president, Kevin Sweeney, came on the line. I had never met him, but I soon came to respect him. He was agile and smart. "What's the deal on this $64,000 challenge?" I asked.

"The deal," he said, "is that we will put up $64,000 to go with a department store's $32,000, making a $96,000 pot. We're going to test radio sales item for item against the same amount of money put in newspapers and see who wins."

"I like it," I said. "We'll do it with Higbee's."

"You're too late," he said. "We're all set with Filene's in Boston." Ugh, I hate rejection! I decided to fight.

"What does Filene's know about radio?" I asked. "They won't help you win. They'll show you how to lose. Higbee's is the department store you should team up with. They are already sold on radio."

Sweeney wasn't an easy sell. He had already gone a long way with Filene's, but he said he'd see me if I came to New York. I was on a plane the next day. A $96,000 radio budget and a challenge from the radio industry were worth pursuing. Of course, I told him about Higbee's successes with radio. He knew that Cleveland radio was hot and that Wyse was an agency that understood how to be creative with radio, especially after our nationwide success with the Bonne Bell 10-0-6 lotion test.

Sweeney and his associate, Miles David, came to Cleveland and interrogated our little staff. By then, we had ten people, including two writers, a broadcast producer, and a media buyer. They all passed inspection, and Higbee's was finally picked as the store to take The $64,000 Challenge. Fortunately, Kevin and Miles had never met the president of Higbee's, Ed Hoffman. I was elated at getting the assignment from the RAB and so was the store ad manager, Marc Jonas. However, when we went to Hoffman to allocate $32,000 for the test, he turned us down flat.

"No," he said. "I don't think it'll work." Unsurprisingly, he added, "If I had an extra $32,000, I'd put it in the newspapers."

I was crushed. I found myself in an untenable position. After selling my heart out on Higbee's great belief in radio came this stupid rebuff. What would I tell Kevin Sweeney? This was the ultimate insult to the radio industry. Hoffman refused their $64,000. I couldn't face Sweeney with this news. I looked Hoffman in the eye and said, "Ed, do you mind if I go under your head."

He looked puzzled. "What do you mean?"

"Let me explain the deal to your four merchandise managers," I responded. "If I can convince them it was what the store should do, will you approve the $32,000 budget?"

Fortunately, he said he would. I had no trouble selling each merchandise manager on the challenge proposition. They saw it as a two-for-one boost in their budgets and were quite happy about it. I never told Sweeney about this situation. He would have given the money to Filene's in a second. It was better for all of us that he never knew about it. As it turned out, the Higbee RAB test was a roaring success for radio. We proved that radio delivered $6 for every $1 spent on advertising, while the same money spent for newspaper advertising for the identical item averaged only a $4 return for each dollar spent. The RAB later published a detailed report on more than 1,000 items we tested. As a result of this test, many department stores and Sears started using radio.

The jingle we wrote for Higbee's was well-remembered by anyone who heard it.

Higbee's is a nice department store.
There are elevators, escalators,
Shoes that once were alligators.
Higbee's is the store with so much more.

Ask any long-time Clevelander to sing the Higbee's jingle, though, and I'll bet 95 percent will give you a fine rendition of the following:

If you haven't seen Higbee's today,
You haven't seen Higbee's.

# 6 | It Takes a Great Client to Buy a Great Campaign

If Willard Smucker had had his way, we never would have worked for the legendary J.M. Smucker Company. They weren't always famous, either. Looking back, we like to think that Wyse Advertising played a little part in getting them to their preeminent status as the Number One fruit spread brand in the U.S. with a 40 percent share of the market. Fortunately, his son Paul and I hit it off immediately. Well, almost immediately.

It was the late '50s, and we had grown our advertising firm to a staff of eight. One of our clients was the annual Food Show in Cleveland. While walking through the show to see some of the exhibits, Lois and I came upon a tiny booth for the Smucker Company. We certainly knew their product well, as we both loved jelly on our toast for breakfast. Their brand was delicious. We also appreciated that it was all manufactured in nearby Orrville, Ohio.

Something about their simple, down-home approach appealed to us. The plain black-and-white labels showing a lady cooking at a wood stove stood out almost as much as their plain, little booth did at the show, surrounded by the colorful displays of the behemoth food companies. I had a gut instinct that this was a small family business just laden with potential and in need of greater visibility in the market.

I saw something else going on with the company that I knew would have a significant impact on their future growth and success. Willard had taken the reigns in the early '30s, when his father, J.M., had reached his 70s and preferred serving as chairman and vacationing in Florida in the winter. A Mennonite farmer, Jerome M. Smucker started the company by picking apples in his Orville orchards, then cooking and selling crocks full of apple butter — and later jams — to his neighbors.

Willard had a reputation as a hard worker, so he was a natural to take over for his dad and move the mom-and-pop operation into a full-fledged business. He gave the company its foundation by setting up production lines, food broker representation, a sales department, and a full line of 43 fruit preserves. As a teenager, his son, Paul, loaded trucks and learned the business the hard way from his taskmaster father. Paul learned where and how to buy fruit. He learned about glass jars and resealing caps. He learned about hiring and firing people. But most important of all, Paul learned about quality, which was fiercely ingrained in the Smucker family culture. That quality extended beyond the product and wrapped around the company's treatment of employees.

In 1959, it extended to shareholders, as the company was taken public by McDonald & Company, a Cleveland-based brokerage and investment firm. By that time, J.M.'s children, Willard, Wilma and Winna, all needed to identify the worth of their pieces of the family business, so they decided to become a public company and thus make it all clear to the Internal Revenue Service, as well. Willard and Paul, now managing directors of the Smucker Company, agonized over the price of each share that McDonald & Co. should guarantee. They drove from Orville to Cleveland to set the final deal. Finally, Willard resolved that the price should be $20 and prepared exhaustive arguments to support his position. He was ready and all pumped up when they entered Burt McDonald's office. Burt greeted them with Bob Hays, the partner who had put the deal together.

Burt spoke first: "We've decided to guarantee you $20 per share." Willard's mouth was open, but nothing came out. This was the beginning of a very profitable relationship for the family and thousands of shareholders.

That's where I came in. I made a cold telephone call to Paul, and I asked if I could come down and meet him to inform him of our company's exceptional abilities in the food business. As my heavy-hitting lead, I cited our experience with Stouffer's Frozen Foods.

"We don't do any advertising," Paul said. "But if you're ever in the neighborhood, please drop in."

Two weeks later, I happened to be in the neighborhood.

Orrville, Ohio, is a little town. It's about fifty miles southwest of Cleveland, somewhere between Akron and Massillon, and has been the hometown of Smucker's since 1897. They were still using the family's original wood-frame house for their offices.

I met with Paul. We had a good time just talking. We liked each other. He reminded me, however, that they just weren't advertising-minded. Out of kindness, he took me to meet his father. As he sat there puffing on a big cigar, Willard gave me a crusty stare. He always seemed crusty. Later, I was to learn this was just a put on. He was really a sweet man. "What do you do?" he asked.

"I'm in advertising."

"Humph, advertising." he responded, throwing back his shoulders. "All advertising men are crooks."

Having your life's work impugned so thoroughly gives you pause. I asked him why he thought so. "I gave that McCann, Erickson $30,000 once," he replied. "Nothing happened. Nothing!"

That's how it all started. Fortunately for me, Paul didn't share his father's beliefs, which, as he emphatically informed me that day, were: "Make a good product. Put it on the shelves. It will sell. You don't need advertising."

Now remember, this was an era that is often referred to as the Golden Age of Advertising. During that time, America's population was 150 million, roughly half of what it is today. The average annual household salary was $3,000. You could mail a letter for 3 cents and buy a gallon of gas for 23 cents. A loaf of bread cost 14 cents, and a jar of jam cost 50 cents, which, the Smuckers will tell you today, was certainly underpriced for the time!

Anyway, when we went back to Paul's office that day, he gave me a grin and a shrug, regarding his father's lecture. He called Wally Clouser, his affable sales manager, into his office and introduced us. We discussed their marketing strategy in greater detail. Before leaving I asked if we could make a formal presentation to show them what advertising could do for Smucker's. In light of his father's philosophy, Paul felt that would be a waste of time for all involved. However, I kept in touch with Paul, and after a while he and Wally agreed to meet more of our people. A few weeks later, Lois, Herb Kanzel, a Wyse copywriter, Patty Rowe, a freelance actress, and I piled into my Nash Rambler, drove to Smucker's and announced ourselves as "The Wyse Players." Paul and Wally were expecting a dry, boring presentation with a lot of facts and figures. Instead, we put on a hysterical, 20-minute play about a postmaster from the Orville post office harassed about huge amounts of mail now arriving in his office all addressed to the Smucker Company.

We sang: "Smucker jelly, Smucker jam. Made the town what it am. Smucker's put Orville on the map."

Paul and Wally howled with laughter. Despite the fun they had that morning, they still weren't ready to go into advertising. Paul turned down our proposal for a radio campaign. Six months later, though, he called from Orville.

"Can you come down?" he said. "I might have an assignment for you."

He explained that Smucker's was building a plant in Salinas, California, and they only had enough orders to keep the plant going one day a week. I learned later that in 1959, Paul had taken responsibility for establishing the Salinas operation and ensuring that it would be successful, despite an unspoken belief within the company that Orville should be the only manufacturing center. So, knowing they needed West Coast business to make this work, Paul thought perhaps running a few "modest" ads out there would garner more orders.

I drove down to Orville, my car quickly becoming accustomed to the trip. "Maybe we could try some FM radio?" Paul suggested. He had this magnificent budget of $75 per week, and Paul and I both knew we needed some resourceful thinking. To begin with, our mighty but little agency couldn't afford to send even one person to California with that budget. Lois and I had been planning a vacation, but weren't sure where we wanted to go. So we chose Salinas. Our sightseeing included the nearly finished Smucker plant. We were admitted by the night watchman and Vernon Netzly, whom Paul had dispatched from Orville to manage the new plant.

Since we didn't have much to spend, we wanted to maximize the impact of our ads by making sure they were well-positioned in the newspapers or on the radio stations' time schedules. So, early on, Smucker's West Coast salesman Don Graber and I visited Sacramento to call on the food editor and staff of the *Sacramento Bee*. We told them the Smucker's story, and we sweetened it with many product samples. We also met with the manager and announcers of the radio station. Then we moved on to Fresno. At each stop, we were surprised that they were surprised and pleased by our personal visits and attention. They weren't used to it. So it was no surprise that we received good time and space placement complemented by some positive, friendly news coverage, as well.

Several months later, Smucker's invited all of the regional food editors to a pancake breakfast and plant tour to celebrate the opening of the plant in Salinas. They had a great time, and the Californians found something charming about the earnest, affable folks from Orrville, Ohio. For the most part, I was having a great time. I believe we secured our relationship with Smucker's by demonstrating our philosophy that we were more than just a consultant who shows up once in a while to present advertising concepts. We were willing to roll up our sleeves and become part of the company's team, if we needed to, and that's what I had done by joining their sales efforts to establish a viable presence in California.

Of course, things didn't always go smoothly. One day while we were attending a party at one of our farmer's homes, something I ate didn't agree with me. I think it was a piece of cake or pie. I went out to the yard to use the farmer's outhouse, and while I was inside, one of the side shutters popped open, and a giant cow poked his head into the window. It scared me to death, as I wasn't expecting any visitors. In the distance, I could hear Paul's raucous laughter, when they came outside and saw my new bovine buddy. I regained some of my status, though, when we went fishing in San Francisco Bay later in the trip, trolling the waters surrounding Alcatraz Prison, and I was the only one who caught any fish.

Resourceful became a common theme when deciding on Smucker's ad budgets. So, Wally Clouser organized a group of Smucker's salesmen we called "The Flying Squadron." He knew that all of our advertising efforts would be wasted if customers couldn't find the products on their grocery store shelves. I joined the group, too. Then Wally planned and led a massive, all-out effort for us to call on the large-chain buyers on the West Coast and food stores all over Northern California. We had to get orders for the new plant. And we did! The Smucker's brand was showing up on a lot of new shelves. Our newspaper and radio ads ran in Sacramento, Fresno, and San Francisco where we had distribution. The Salinas plant, according to Vernon, could now operate two days a week.

Radio advertising became the big part of Smucker's resourceful budget. We bought time on Gene Autry's radio station, KMPC in Los Angeles.

Smucker's benefitted when the Safeway chain bought its jelly supplier in Oakland and created an opening for Smucker's with other major West Coast chains that refused to do business with a Safeway subsidiary. We also bought radio time in Cleveland, Columbus, Indianapolis, Detroit, and Toledo. The tiny Smucker's Company, with only $9 million in annual sales, was starting to grow. Kraft jelly was the major competitor. They were on national television with Perry Como. We had to counter that because Smucker's had growing distribution in many parts of the country. Only the East Coast and the Deep South were devoid of the Smucker's brand. We needed big-time credibility, so we bought time on the Gary Moore Show on the CBS Radio Network. Kraft had Perry Como; we had Gary Moore. We were excited to tell our food brokers and the grocery trade about it. It made no difference that Kraft was spending $5 million and we were spending $300,000.

When we first launched our business relationship with Paul, he set the goal for us to help Smucker's sales grow from $9 million a year to $12 million in just over two years. We achieved that goal in 18 months. On that day, Paul and I went to Orville's Manhattan restaurant and had a piece of homemade pie and ice cream. Come to think of it, over the years, Paul and I celebrated over many pieces of homemade pie.

After we had the Smucker's account for about four years, sales were going well, and the company had entered several other markets in the U.S. We even got Willard to concede that the advertising "isn't hurting." Things were fine and growing in the West and Midwest, but we still hadn't broken into the biggest market of all: New York City. Paul asked us to devise a campaign for New York and the tough East Coast markets. Lois and I knew there was one potential obstacle. The name Smucker did slightly sound like a certain ethnic epithet popular in the Big Apple. We also knew, however, that the name was never going to change, especially since it was considered a great family name in Orville, along with Hofstetler, Yoder, and Zoot.

Around that same time, Lois and I attended an Advertising Age Creative Seminar in Chicago. We were particularly impressed by one of the speakers who headed up an agency in San Francisco. His name was Howard Gossage. His work was outstanding and inspirational. "Challenge your creative department to find the difference," he said. "Every client is unique. Even if the products seem alike, they're not. Make the effort to locate the idea that will distinguish your client." The man made a lot of sense.

When we got back to our hotel room, Lois and I talked about Gossage. We discussed how we had this amazing client, and they needed to break into the biggest market in the country. Right there, I challenged her to write a great radio spot for Smucker's.

"Oh yeah," she said. "I could write it, but you couldn't sell it."

I pointed to her pink portable typewriter which she always brought along with her. "Let's see you write it," I said.

She sat down and typed furiously. In 60 seconds she wrote a 60-second spot for radio that would double as an ad for print. Triumphantly she pulled the paper from the typewriter and handed it to me with a dramatic flourish. I sat down and read it. I read it twice. There it was: "WITH A NAME LIKE SMUCKER'S, IT HAS TO BE GOOD. If we're going to make up a name for a jelly, would we call it Smucker's? Not on your life. We'd call it Gramma's Best or Ye Olde Jam Pot. But we call it Smucker's because that's our family name. The company was started by our grandfather in 1897. And we're proud of that. And we're proud of the preserves that we put in the jar. That's why we call it Smucker's."

I loved it. I told her I thought it was fantastic, but she just laughed and said, "You'll never do anything with it." Ha. I couldn't wait to get to Orville. A few days later, I was there. I was in the conference room which occupied the entire second floor of a narrow but neat wooden building above the company's offices. Paul Smucker and Wally Clouser listened while I read the spot. When I was finished I was greeted with silence. And darkness. Willard preferred to spend money on plant production, not office lighting, so I couldn't quite read their faces. After an awkward little pause, Wally finally spoke.

"Are you kidding?" he said. "If we run that, we'll be laughed out of town."

"Wait a minute," interrupted Paul. "Marc," he said. "Do you think that commercial will sell jelly?"

"Look, Paul," I reasoned. "Don't people sometimes kid you about your name?"

"Some," he said.

"Well, then, let's have some fun with it ourselves. After all we're only trying to sell them a little jelly. We're not trying to end the war in Vietnam or anything serious like that."

"OK," said Paul. Then he hesitated. "But . . ."

"But what?" I asked.

"Well," he said. "You know my relatives around here might object. But, if you think it'll help us sell jelly, let's run it on the West Coast where we don't have any relatives."

So that's where it all started in 1962 on radio in Los Angeles, Fresno, Sacramento, and San Francisco. Six weeks later, Paul boarded an American Airlines flight to Los Angeles at the Cleveland airport. Remember how the flight attendant used to check your name as you buckled up? Paul Smucker gave his name. Immediately, the attendant said, "Oh! With a name like Smucker's, it has to be good!" In fact, everywhere Paul traveled on the West

Coast people kept smiling and repeating the slogan to him, including the chain grocery buyers with whom he met.

When he returned to Orville, Paul called me on the phone all enthused. "Marc, run that spot in New York. Heck, run those commercials all over the country."

"What about the relatives?" I said.

"Hang the relatives," he said. "They'll be happy with the dividend checks."

We launched the New York campaign with a somewhat modest $50,000 budget. We coupled the radio commercial with an introductory offer. Customers could mail the jar label back to Orrville for a rebate. New Yorkers quickly fell for the slogan "With a name like Smucker's...," and we were on our way on the East Coast. If I do say so myself, it remains one of the true super slogans of advertising, making a strange and funny sounding name that grocers, housewives, and husbands usually misspelled into a household word. Half a century later, it remains the main theme of Smucker's advertising.

One night, when the company sponsored part of "The Johnny Carson Show," even television's most famous late night host uttered the ubiquitous slogan: "With a name like Smucker's, it has to be good. And they make more than preserves and jellies. Here's Ed to show you and tell you about Smucker's." His sidekick Ed McMahon then tried to put scoops of ice cream into a bowl and place Smucker's chocolate topping on them. "Yes! I hope you're a lot neater than I am, but lots of topping, lots of ice cream, and it looks something like that, friends. You'll have a real treat. That will keep you going for the whole show tonight."

In those days, commercials were filmed live on TV. The commercial went off just fine, but afterwards Carson kept trying to get Ed McMahon to eat the chocolate sundae he had just created. McMahon politely refused. "You said it was so great," Carson pressed. "Why don't you eat it?"

"Because I made it. I'd feel funny eating it myself," McMahon countered. "You ought to have it." Both men were holding back laughter, until it got so ridiculous that they had to explain. Ice cream melts quickly under the hot studio lights, McMahon pointed out to viewers. Therefore, television programs usually substitute a Crisco-like, vegetable-based substance to represent ice cream in commercials. The segment closed with a sheepish McMahon wondering, "Where will I be working tomorrow?"

After that night, Smucker's developed a new ground rule for studio technicians: When shooting a Smucker topping commercial, use as many takes and as many pounds of melted ice cream as necessary, but no Crisco!

For us, the Smucker Company represents the ideal client. Being a good client is not easy. It takes imagination, sensibility, and often courage. It wasn't easy for Paul Smucker to allow us to poke fun at his name when we coined the phrase, "With a name like Smucker's, it has to be good." Can you accept a really new, fresh idea? Do you have the guts to be a pioneer? Do you believe that somebody else can have a great idea for your business? Good clients know that if they have to tell their advertising agency what to do, they should get themselves another agency. They also know that once they've hired an agency with some intelligence, creativity, marketing savvy, and backbone, they should sit down with them and set forth a statement of goals. Agree on the long-term and short-term objectives. Then spell it all out with a roadmap on how they're going to get where they want to go. Take an honest look at their company's strengths and weaknesses. Take an honest look at their competitors' strengths and weaknesses. Agree on the positioning of their company in the marketplace. Then sit back and give good advertising professionals the opportunity to perform.

I must tell you, too, that working in a small town like Orville, you remember what America's values are all about. When you are employed by a company like Smucker's, you're proud to work for a business right out of America's great heartland, with people who are devoted to quality with a passion and who possess a proud, four-generation family tradition of running a solid company. Smucker's goals and objectives were clearly defined. So was its personality. Smucker's felt that everything they did must have a quality feel. This meant their packaging, their trade policies, and their advertising. They realized that their main competition was the supermarket chains' own private label brands and the two giants Kraft and Welch. In most places, Smucker's cost a little more per jar, so they had to sell as a better value to Mrs. Consumer. Smucker's couldn't and didn't want to sell price.

Smucker's advertising had to be distinctive. It really couldn't be anything a chain could run and least of all one of the giant competitors. Above all, it had to be honest. I observed the company very closely, and I recognized they were not like any other jelly company. They were in truth a wonderful family running this wonderful little jelly company in Orville, Ohio... since 1897... in the American tradition of quality and home cooking. Both Lois and I agreed that consumers wanted to believe their preserves were carefully cooked by nice family people in a small town in Ohio, rather than by machines in some slick plant in Chicago.

The theme line that Lois had instinctively written fit perfectly. I would go to lunch with Paul, and he would tell me story after story about people who worked at Smucker's and gave the place its family-inspired character. There was Squeak Fulmer, Marlin Icenogle, Iris Bootzer, Daryl McQuilken, Tater Burkholder, and Vernon Netzley to name a few. All of them had names equally distinctive as Smucker. All of these people were proud to work at Smucker's. The emphasis on quality workmanship ingrained a strong sense of proprietorship in each and every employee, as Paul used to say, almost as if it were their own names on the jars. I would come back to the agency and tell these stories to Lois. She did the rest. She sat at her typewriter and wrote very human and homespun copy for our radio ads. Some of the spots were funny. Some were serious. But all of them were honest and memorable. We selected the late Mason Adams to be our voice. Mason isn't an announcer. He's an actor. Years ago, he played "Pepper Young" on CBS radio. You may also remember him as Ed Asner's boss on "Lou Grant," a spinoff from "The Mary Tyler Moore Show." His distinctive, rich voice was perfect to tell these Smucker stories.

A big advantage about putting our money on radio came from the stations and their on-air personalities. They were charmed by the Smucker spots and many of them created Smucker promotions around them. WNEW in New York decided to run a full-page ad in *The New York Times* listing funny names of people sent in by listeners. It was all good natural humor and our client received tons of free publicity.

Our commercial told how Louella Just, Smucker's receptionist and telephone operator, could name all 43 Smucker flavors by heart. Geoff Edwards, a disc jockey on KMPC - Los Angeles, decided to call Louella while he was on the air to see if she could do it. Much to the amazement and amusement of KMPC's 50,000-watt audience, Louella came through perfectly.

Then Geoff asked Louella, "What's the weather like right now in Orville?" "It's snowing," said Louella. "It's like Mother Goose shaking her feathers."

A week later Smucker's received a letter from a native Ohioan now living in Southern California. He had heard Louella's remarks while driving on the hot and congested San Diego Freeway. He made up his mind to return to Ohio.

Of course, a good grocery buyer is trying to get the best deal and the best opportunity for his company. When Smucker's decided to enter Chicago competitor Kraft's hometown, we knew we had to do something special.

We had the funny-name radio commercials, and we decided to back them up with two full-page newspaper ads. When I presented the ads to Paul, he loved them. "But," he asked, "why full-page? Can't we do something smaller?"

"You're too small to run a small ad," I said. "Let your Chicago food broker show these ads and play the radio spots for Jewell. You've got to impress them." Jewell Supermarkets, the biggest food retailer in Chicago, was charmed by the ads, and ordered Smucker's distribution in all their stores.

Big-city markets and big-city supermarket chains are always hard to sell. Their size and buying power often make their buyers a little arrogant. They demand deals and discounts that can be unreasonable and unprofitable to suppliers. The Smucker ethic of fairness and providing the same deal to all often clashed with these tough tactics. Smucker's stood by their principles. The buyer at Giant Supermarkets in Washington, D.C., was highly aware of his company's dominance in the market. For many years, Smucker sales representatives tried to sell Giant. However, this buyer's demands for free cases and payment terms exceeded Smucker's normal introductory allowances. They stood firm and to this day they don't have a Smucker's jar at Giant. I always admired Smucker's for that. I was very proud to represent them.

Wyse was the Smucker agency for 35 years. Our people saw them grow from a 1 percent share to a 40 percent share of the jelly and preserve business. Their annual sales volume went from $9 million to more than $500 million a couple decades later. It was exciting to have played a role in this great American business success. Although I am no longer active in Wyse Advertising, I continue my relationship with Paul's sons, Richard and Tim, who continue to lead the Smucker business. They are now cultivating the fifth generation of Smuckers to lead the company deep into the 21st century.

Paul Smucker was one of the greatest men I have ever met. He had integrity, and he was the most ethical, fine person. Everything you feel about Smucker's, the package, the commercials, the integrity is there. Much of it was inspired by Paul's wife, Lorraine, who was also just a great person.

I spoke to the Smucker boys recently. Richard reiterated how by working closely with their father, Paul, we helped establish the brand to be known nationwide. "Obviously, a lot of good times were shared in terms of business and personal experiences," he said.

"In the annals of business relationships, this has got to be one of the longest, with a lifelong friendship, too," Tim added. "It certainly benefitted our companies, our respective brands and our employees."

Under their exceptional leadership, the J.M. Smucker Company has continued to grow their market share, acquiring such products as Crisco vegetable oil, Jif peanut butter, Hungry Jack dry grocery products, Pillsbury flour, and Folgers coffee. As the company has grown, they have never veered from the philosophies of manufacturing and selling the highest-quality products and holding to honest, ethical business practices originally established by J. M. Smucker. They are also the best clients an agency ever had.

# 7 | There's No Such Thing as No!

In business, everyone should have a dream. To obtain that dream, though, you need to be tenacious. You need to learn how to push past obstacles, and how to get beyond the word "No" from a client or potential client by being persistent and coming back to them with new approaches until they say "Yes." We did it time and again at Wyse Advertising, and by doing so we landed some of our biggest and best clients. Early on, one of the dream achievements for me was to win the East Ohio Gas Company account. In fact, I held it up as my "impossible dream." I believe I gave the utility company such high esteem as a possible client because of some of my most cherished childhood memories.

When I was growing up, we had a large porcelain white gas stove in the kitchen that my mother used masterfully to cook and bake all kinds of delicious meals for our family. I was always fascinated with the rings of blue flame that sprang off the burner when she lit a wooden match over it. She regulated the gas intake valve with one hand and then the flame with her other hand.

That old gas range seemed like the lifeline of our household. It went on first thing in the morning to fry the eggs, and it went off late at night after boiling water for my father's tea and Schnapps. In winter, our coal furnace was a nightmare, even when we could afford the coal. Our house was always freezing, so many days Mom would light the gas oven. Then, she would open the oven door and heat up our tiny, little kitchen. On the coldest days of those brutal Cleveland winters, it was the one warm room in our home.

Once a month, Mom would pay the gas bill. She would take me with her on the Kinsman street car. When we got downtown, we'd walk over to the gas company at 1405 East Sixth Street. I remember the massive marble columns and our echoing footsteps in the gas building lobby. I remember the friendly guards and the nice ladies behind the cashier windows. The bill would get stamped "paid." All of this would cost about $4, and in those days, $4 was $4. I found out later that my father was making about $40 a week.

Why my mother had to trudge all the way down to the gas company office, I never knew. She could have paid the bill by mail or at a neighborhood bank, but she didn't trust that. Paying the gas bill was too important. She saved the paid bills in a drawer for years. She said, "They take care of us."

Those were my first impressions of the East Ohio Gas Company. When you turned on the gas, it was there. We got to know the East Ohio Gas Company as one of the most caring, sensitive, aggressive, and responsible companies in Northeast Ohio. And you know something? It still is.

At our agency, we didn't start pitching for the East Ohio account until we had enough staff to properly serve it. I knew it was going to take a long time. I knew it was going to prove a lesson in tenacity. I made call after call. I even outlasted three administrations. They kept saying, "No." I kept saying, "Why not?" Finally they started saying, "Maybe." Then I knew I was close. It had only taken 18 years to get the East Ohio Gas account. Dudley Taw, the president, Ray Ernest, the marketing director, and Charlie Eder, the advertising manager, with solid poker faces, called me into their office one morning and offered me their account. I cried a little. At last, me, the kid from Kinsman, I had my impossible dream.

East Ohio was a regulated utility. They were part of the Consolidated Natural Gas System that was based in Pittsburgh. A lot of people don't understand utilities. Some businesspeople scoff at their marketing programs. "Marketing," they say. "Why do they need marketing? They don't have any competition." Some consumers complain. "They can charge anything they want. They're the only gas company that is connected to my house." All of these naive observations confront utilities every day. There are plenty of competition and government regulators constantly policing them. The marketing mission is often contrary logic. Sometimes utilities ask their customers to use less of their energy because of shortages or inflationary run-ins with government regulators. That's what happened in the '70s, and it resulted in a lot of poor people having a tough time paying their gas bill. The message we had to send was "Conserve. Use gas sparingly. Save money." We had to find a way to convey that message quickly and effectively. It was especially important for the inner-city black community.

Then I found it. A good friend of mine, Joe Zingale, had met comedy and entertainment superstar Bill Cosby in Las Vegas. Born and raised in the projects of Philadelphia, William H. Cosby, Jr., went on to enjoy a wildly successful, five-decade career as a stand-up comedian, TV and film star, author, educator, and philanthropist. He won numerous Gold and Platinum records and Grammy Awards for his extremely popular comedy albums. In the mid-1960s, shortly after the Civil Rights Act had passed, his role in the hit TV program "I Spy" made him the first African-American to co-star in a dramatic series, and his performances earned him three Emmy Awards. Of course, years later, his family sitcom "The Cosby Show" became one of the most highly watched shows on television ever.

On the personal side, one of Cosby's favorite pastimes was tennis; over the years, he and Zingale had played tennis together many times in Las Vegas and became close friends. By a lucky coincidence, Cosby was booked to appear in person at Greater Cleveland's Front Row Theater. I was excited by the possibility of enlisting him in as a highly respected spokesman in our cause. What if? No, it's impossible. But why not try? So I did. I found out from Joe that Cosby was staying at the Downtown Motor Inn at East 18th Street and Euclid. It was 9 a.m. on a Saturday morning, and my phone call reached him in his room. I must have awakened him.

"You want me to do what?" he said

"I want you to do a commercial for East Ohio Gas."

"East Ohio who?"

"Gas. East Ohio Gas," I said.

"Why should I do a commercial for the East Ohio Gas Company? Do you know how much Ford Motor Company is paying me to do commercials?"

"No."

"$750,000. Do you know how much Jell-O is paying me?"

"No."

"$450,000. You tell me why I should do a commercial for the East Ohio Gas Company."

"We don't have that kind of money to spend. Not even near that," I explained. "But I have a better reason."

"What's that?" he said.

"The people in the black community here need you," I said. "Somebody they can believe has to tell them to turn down their thermostats so they can save money on their gas bills."

There was silence on the other end of the line. Then he said very quietly, "When do you want me to tape these commercials?"

Cosby turned out to be a real friend of ours at East Ohio. He was sympathetic to our messages and extremely cooperative. We provided him a rough script telling what we wanted each spot to convey, and then he put it in his own words and style. Some people asked: Why are you using Cosby as a spokesman for East Ohio? Is it because he's funny? Is it because he's lovable and that would rub off on us? Is it because he's black and that's a popular thing to do today? Why?

Despite East Ohio's best efforts and "lean over backwards" policies, it was getting tougher and tougher to retain the good will of the public. The politicians, the newspapers and the broadcast newscasters had a vendetta out to get all business. Banks and utilities were prime targets. Sometimes they forget what it is that makes our country great. People are also suspicious of business. They talk about a business's high profits, but they forget to talk about its huge investments and risks. They talk about a business's growth and expansion as if they were onerous things, but they forget that they mean opportunity to create more jobs and increase people development for employees at all levels.

The reason we hired Bill Cosby was that he made our advertising as honest and as believable as it could get. He wouldn't say anything on those commercials unless he believed every word. He made us prove all statements to him first. That's why the spots worked.

People in the business asked me, "How did you get Cosby to do those spots? He's on for Ford, Jell-O, and now East Ohio Gas. How could you afford him?" All we had to do was convince him that he was doing the right thing. He's a good person. He cares about people. His immense talents deserve all the money he's ever made. But to Cosby, helping people is always more important than money.

# 8 | When You're Hot, You're Hot

When you are in the advertising agency business in Cleveland, Ohio, major advertisers look at you cross-eyed. That was true in 1967 as well as today. Of course, there are some exceptions, especially when those advertisers are headquartered in the Northern Ohio area. BP America, Goodyear, Sherwin-Williams, Smucker's, Stouffer's, and TRW Inc. had their corporate headquarters here and were all Wyse clients, but we longed for the big time. That meant New York. I sometimes wonder how big and successful we could have been had we started in Manhattan.

We certainly weren't unhappy. We were living in lovely Shaker Heights, Ohio. Our business was successful by any standard. Smucker's alone had grown to annual sales of $40 million and was spending nearly $2 million yearly in advertising, mostly on network television. But by 1967, after 16 years in Cleveland, we felt that we had expanded our agency just about as far as we could. A location in New York would place us at the heart of the greatest talent pool and finest production facilities in the world, as well as in the midst of countless corporate headquarters. NY, NY, represented an ideal location, if we wanted to be close to new sources of business. So, in February of that year, we acquired an existing agency to launch our New York branch. Within 18 months, we had grown our creative staff from three to twenty-one people, each specializing in a particular medium — television, radio, or print — added high-profile clients such as Consolidated Foods, Endocil beauty products, Longchamp's restaurant chain, Piaget watches, R.J. Reynolds Foods, and United Jewish Appeal, and increased our billings by $5 million to $10 million total.

How did the expansion come about, you ask? One day Lois and I were introduced to George Elliot, who had been an art director at McCann-Erickson, New York. George was brilliant. He was an enormous talent. He was strategic and had incredible insights on human behavior and needs. His graphic skills were even more remarkable. They were simple, beautiful, and passed along powerful messages. George was frustrated by the political atmosphere and the client restrictions at McCann. At his resignation party, a well-known photographer, Art Kane, gave George a fine camera. That was what he really wanted, and George decided to become a "great" advertising photographer in New York. Modesty was not among George's finer virtues. For Lois and me, George became a teacher and an exciting friend. Lois would say, "George stretches my brain and makes me a better writer." I would say, "George, I love what you do, and I could sell it."

Working together with George, we sold several campaigns. Two of them won the Best in Show Awards in two successive years for the Cleveland Society of Communicating Arts competition. One award was for Old Times Ale and five others for Higbee's Department Store. The Cleveland advertising community was stunned. They wondered how a nine-person agency could walk away with the top awards. Wyse was beginning to build its creative reputation. Lois, who had worked as a highly disciplined journalist for *The Cleveland Press*, became a phenomenal ad writer. She worked very fast. After a client briefing, she'd return to the office and have an entire campaign written in about an hour. I would wait a couple of days before I brought the work to the client. I didn't want them to think it was that easy.

Working with George became more difficult because he became very busy as a photographer. He was so successful that he was planning to buy the building that he occupied for his studio. Lois and I were building our own creative staff in Cleveland, as our business was rapidly expanding. We were able to attract outstanding graphic and writing talent. We continued to grow and continued to dominate the local award shows.

Sadly, we learned one day that George had been killed in a small plane air accident on a photo assignment for the U.S. Army in Florida. But George had given us a large taste of New York art talent, and we looked for other sources.

As Smucker's continued to expand, we faced major competition from Kraft jellies, who were co-sponsors of the Perry Como show on national television. As I mentioned earlier, we countered with the Gary Moore Show on network radio. His show was on CBS, and that's why I got a call from Herb Lubalin, the fabulous New York art director who had been a partner of Sudler, Hennessy and Lubalin, a well-known New York agency. CBS radio network was their client, and Herb was assigned to a trade ad announcing the new Smucker's CBS radio relationship. I had negotiated a free merchandise package from CBS. This trade ad was one piece of that.

Lois and I met Lubalin and were enthralled with this little bird-faced man whose creative talents soared with eagles. He created all types of layouts and typefaces. He designed packages and displays that were unique and new that seemed to be fashioned from the nostalgic past. Lubalin was sweet, witty, and caustic, all at the same time. He looked at advertising from an artist's standpoint. "Advertising stinks," he would say as he criticized bad clients who forced supplicant agencies into bad campaigns. Lubalin was small of stature but he was a giant of a man.

"What are you two guys doing in Cleveland?" he said to Lois and me. "You belong in New York."

Herb had us meet Arthur Sudler, the president of Sudler & Hennessy, for dinner at the Lotos Club on East 66th Street in Manhattan, one of the oldest literary clubs in America. Mr. Samuel L. Clemens (Mark Twain) joined in 1873, three years after the club opened. Shortly after we all tucked into our mouthwatering meals, Arthur told us that he wanted to make Sudler & Hennessey an agency that specialized in medical advertising exclusively. He was willing to sell us the consumer advertising part of his business. Lois and I were excited and quickly accepted his offer. This was our opportunity to try our skills in the big city against the foremost competition in our field. Besides, we could work with Lubalin, who had recently opened his own creative studio.

We began with four accounts that had been with Sudler & Hennessey: the CBS Radio Network, General Electric Textolite, Swiss Industries Group, and the Swiss National Tourist Office. The combined total billings were $1 million. It wasn't much of a start, but we only inherited five employees. We had an excellent copywriter, a personable account man, a savvy media lady, a secretary and a receptionist. I felt important when I signed a lease in a New York skyscraper at 845 Third Avenue. I had my own office in Manhattan. I could hardly believe it. Herb Lubalin was retained as our "as needed" art director, so we were ready to do business.

It didn't take long. I learned that Angostura-Wupperman, manufacturer of Angostura Bitters, was looking for an ad agency. I reached Bill Dey, their advertising manager, and we scheduled a lunch date. It was magic. We liked each other immediately. He was an athlete, and so was I. He had gone to Dartmouth, and so had I. Picking an ad agency isn't easy. All of them have good success stories, creative awards, and outstanding people. Bill had meticulously interviewed about ten agencies, and lucky for Wyse, the chemistry between me and Bill was just right. He introduced me to his president, who approved his selection. Just four weeks after we had opened our office, we had our newest account, Angostura Bitters.

Angostura is a very unique product. It is primarily a sophisticated flavor enhancer for food and drinks. At that time, they controlled 95 percent of their market. The market, however, was very small. Although it is readily on hand in many kitchens and bars, most drinks require only a few drops. We found that, because it was sold in eight-ounce quantities, an Angostura bottle can remain on a user's shelf for as long as eight years. We decided to promote the fact that bitters could be used as seasoning in cooking. Our first ad that appeared in Sunday's *New York Times Magazine* read, "No wonder we're bitter." The campaign was written by Byron Barkley and designed by Herb Lubalin and featured a write-in offer for a free cookbook. The campaign got rave reviews. It started to spark Angostura's business, as sales increased considerably. Bill Dey was ecstatic, and then for some unknown reason, the president hired a marketing director. Bill was told to report to him, and naturally he had his own ideas about advertising. In frustration, Bill resigned from the company. I liked Bill, and as our New York office started to prosper, I asked him to join us.

We also had a great find in Judy West, who headed our media buying department and because of her fun antics was known as the "chief kook" in the office. A former big-band singer, she had come from Sudler & Hennessey, and prior to that, she had worked for Politz marketing research for several years. She believed that unless a buyer had a strong background in marketing, he or she could be dazzled by the numbers. The most important thing for a buyer, she felt, was what the numbers mean in terms of how the buyer could make someone more receptive to a particular medium. They have to understand that a medium can offer different audiences, as well. For example, *The New York Times* is one paper during the week and another on Sunday; the audience for a morning television program is quite different from the audience for soap operas in the afternoon, which is different still from the audience for primetime TV shows. That's why women's hygiene products were more likely to be advertised during the afternoon soaps, so that the women would be less likely to be embarrassed in front of their husbands or kids. Because the women knew the programs were for them, they tended to have more faith in them and thus in the advertising, Judy said. During primetime, she believed that you can't just consider the numbers alone, but you have to look at the content. In other words, you wouldn't run a soft spot during a violent show.

One of the New York office's strengths was that Judy and her media staff worked hand-in-hand with our creative staff. Before the creative work was finished for a client, she and her staff would develop a comprehensive market plan. The creative department loved it, because it enabled them to tailor the spots to the exact audience as planned. Conversely, the media staff would shape their plan to accommodate who the creative folks were designing the spots for in the advertising campaign.

Through a friend of Lois we met an incredible personality, John Johnson, the black owner and publisher of *Ebony* and *Jet* magazines. We were assigned the *Ebony* account, and we ran a series of full-page ads in the daily *New York Times*. Herb Lubalin and Byron Barkley created the ads. They were outstanding and immediately put Wyse on the Madison Avenue map. They took first place in the prestigious New York ANDY Awards Show sponsored by The Advertising Club of New York. One ad showed a typically embittered Southern redneck with a half-chewed cigar clenched in his teeth. The headline read, "Some of our best friends are bigots." The copy explained, "Give us a bigot every time, as long as they understand what a big influential market our black readers represent. What we don't need are these do-good liberals who pat us on the back but forget we need to be and deserve to be padded in the pocket book."

After the *Ebony* success, John invited Lois and me to Chicago to handle the advertising for his line of cosmetics. He met us at O'Hare airport and was waiting for us in a big black Cadillac limousine. We were surprised to see John in the driver's seat. He was laughing when we got in the car.

"What's so funny, John?" I asked of our millionaire chauffeur.

"That cop," he pointed out. "He just asked me if my boss knew I was driving his car without a chauffeur's hat."

"That bothers you doesn't it, John?"

"Naw," he said as he drove out of the airport. "I love stupid cops."

John Johnson remained a good friend for a long time. We admired his novel ideas, his ambitions, and his ability to find humor in any situation. We attended his beauty clinics and fashion shows all over the country. He had our utmost respect.

Soon other business appeared, and we moved to larger offices at 777 Third Avenue. We hired a new full-time creative director, Dick Voehl, and a writer, Alan Saperstein, as assignments multiplied. Only 29, Voehl was a graduate of the prestigious Rhode Island School of Design and had worked in advertising for six years. Larry Wassong was also 29 with six years of advertising experience when he joined us from Doyle, Dane, Bernbach to head our account services. Saperstein, then 24, had worked for Needham, Harper & Steers and Benton & Bowles; Voehl admired the young writer's approach to creative problems, so he named him copy chief. Our New York team was in place, and we were hot! Larry connected on the Larry Elman restaurants. He had sold the Cattleman and L'Orangerie. We pleased CBS Radio Network, and they added WCBS, their New York Flagship Station, which was introducing an all-news format with a substantial budget.

Voehl, Saperstein and their creative staff began winning awards and new clients with their imaginative print ads. For starters, the venerable Catskills resort area was struggling to attract new visitors, since younger people thought of the region as someplace old-fashioned, dowdy, and the ideal vacation spot for their grandparents. Voehl teamed with writer Jerry Silverman to devise the concept of calling the Catskills an island. "Announcing a new island. Right off the coast of New York City" that offers everything any other island could, except its much closer and easier to get to. The single-page, black-and-white ad they ran in *The New York Sunday Times Sunday Magazine* drew a record 1,500 responses from a single insertion and later became a finalist for an ANDY Award. Silverman and Voehl partnered again on another ANDY finalist, their creative efforts for GE's Textolite division, which manufactured a plastic similar to the then-omnipresent Formica®. "The War Against Ugly" campaign also helped Textolite increase its market share from 13 percent to 20 percent. For the United Jewish Appeal, Voehl and Saperstein's "Peace is Hell" and "The 365-Day War" ads became ANDY finalists, and Wyse's campaign for the Swiss National Tourist Office elevated Switzerland from the sixth most visited destination to the first, according to U.S. Passport statistics. We were also very proud of our agency's work for Cavanagh's, a 98-year-old steakhouse in the Longchamp's chain. The campaign helped increase their business an astonishing 60 percent in the first month, which happened to be in mid-summer, a traditionally slow period for restaurants in New York, when everyone leaves town for their homes on Long Island or other vacation retreats.

Then, along came the big one: the British Cunard Line. They had just introduced their magnificent new ship, *The Queen Elizabeth II*. The shipping industry was foundering, to say the least. So, we knew that if the *QE2* could turn a profit in the face of increasingly growing competition from commercial airlines, they could become our showcase account. More than 20 ad shops were fighting for the business. Cunard had two serious problems: First, the median age of ship passengers then was 55, so they needed to draw younger customers without losing the majority of the older ones. Second, any effective advertising campaign would have to attract enough passengers to fill the ship on a weekly basis, but it would also have to create a powerful enough image to drive sales for the next decade, while jumbo jets and SSTs emerged as popular forms of transportation.

I was proud to participate with Larry, Dick and Alan in the long elimination series of presentations Cunard put us all through. We devised our campaign to sell the superb ship itself as a destination. As you've probably seen in numerous TV ads highlighting all of their exciting onboard adventures, cruise lines today still use that angle in their advertising. The theme we developed was "The *QE2* versus any vacation in the world." At the presentation, we exhibited ads that demonstrated the many activities available to passengers aboard the ship while on the open sea. Cunard whittled down the agencies, until we were one of six finalists. We made our third and last presentation to the original three executives plus five members of the Board of Directors, who had flown in from Southampton, England. Impressed by what they saw, the team selected us as Cunard's agency, even though the company's president later admitted that he had never heard of Wyse Advertising before the presentations. Roger Pappin, Cunard's advertising manager, and Nick Anderson, vice-president for marketing, became our new clients. They gave us our first assignment: Take a Caribbean Island cruise on the new ship. Yes, I know. A tough task, but we had to do it. Count Basie's Orchestra and Sarah Vaughn entertained us all week. Nevertheless, that campaign represented a true turning point for our New York endeavor, as it convinced Lois and me that Wassong, Voehl and Saperstein could handle their end of the agency quite well.

At one point, a fashion editor at *Harper's Bazaar* told us about Gerry Gedalio, who was the head of North American Watch. His company was the exclusive distributor of Piaget and Corum watches in the U.S. I called him and got an appointment for Lois and me. Gerry was a Cuban with a heavy Spanish accent. Some of his diamond-studded watches sold for more than $10,000. After looking at our work and a half-hour of conversation, Gerry challenged us to write a really great ad for Piaget. This assignment was perfect for Lois. Her copy flowed with sophisticated praise for Piaget, "the most beautiful watch in the world." Gerry loved the ad and the long copy. He ran it as a full-page ad in several magazines. The long copy ad appeared with one small picture of a Piaget Watch. After we got the account, Gerry would only approve ads with several watches and very little copy.

Our staff was young, fresh and a little out of control. One of our writers was Paul Howard. He was the son of Moe Howard of "The Three Stooges" Larry, Curly and Moe fame. Paul loved to dash full speed down the office corridor and slide into an imagined home plate. With Lois and I still living in Cleveland, the office lacked strong leadership. Larry's relationship with

Dick and Alan waned. He left when he ran into personal problems at home. Most of the business left, too.

By this time, Lois was building a second career in publishing. She had written and published 14 books of children's stories and poems for McMillan, Doubleday, and Bantam publishing houses, as well as short stories for *Cosmopolitan, Ladies' Home Journal* and *McCall's*. So naturally she decided to get closer to the publishing world by buying a New York penthouse apartment on East 57th Street. This also positioned Lois to helm our New York Office, and she gave it the talent and leadership it needed. Her first breakthrough was at Revlon. She was hired by the one and only Charles Revson, probably the most difficult client in New York. A cosmetics industry pioneer, Revson founded and managed Revlon for five decades. The assignment for Wyse was to introduce Milk Plus Six Shampoo. Everything anybody ever heard about the mercurial Mr. Charles — good and bad — we experienced in Revlon business meetings. Despite wonderful meetings with Revlon executives, Paul Woolard and Sandy Buchsbaum, the relationship suddenly ended with an inexplicable order from the often irrational Mr. Charles.

The very next week we were hired by Clairol. Lois was perfectly suited to work on Clairol, the leader in hair color. She had long been a Clairol blonde, and she knew how to appeal to women. She wrote a book about blondes, and both Bruce Gelb and Don Shea of Clairol became good clients and also good friends. Dick Voehl's beautiful art direction and Lois's sensitive copy introduced Clairesse. It became one of Clairol's major brands. Wyse hired Cheryl Tiegs as the key Clairesse model, and she and her photographer husband appeared at Wyse New York Christmas parties.

Wyse New York hit its highest peak with the awarding of several Seagram brands. Seagram's Dick Newman, president of a major unit, came to Cleveland for our Wolfschmidt Vodka presentation. The campaign was stunning. Most of it was shot on Virgin Garda Island in the British

West Indies. The island setting at Biras Creek was so incredible that we vacationed there twice.

I always believed that the breadth and diversity of our clientele enhanced the creative spark in our offices, whether Cleveland or New York. Like Larry Wassong once said, "If we had to sell 100 brands of cereal, we could never be as good." Moreover, we never relied on having one giant account that was responsible for half or more of our revenue that would have jeopardized the health of our agency had they chosen to leave.

Of course, in the middle of this flurry of business activity to establish an advertising agency office in New York City, Lois and I were voted "Man and Woman of the Year" by the Cleveland Society of Communication Arts, the city's art directors' club. Quite an honor.

In the early days of Wyse New York, we commuted frequently. Once we were settled in and Lois was running the office, though, I would usually visit for at least a few days every month, sometimes a day or two each week. We never felt it was a problem, especially since we maintained a three-bedroom suite in a townhouse, while our visitors to New York would stay at the Regency Hotel at East 61st Street and Park Avenue, now a Lowe's hotel. Before we had the penthouse, though, I loved to stay at the Regency. The lovely, first-class hotel went out of its way to make you comfortable, and besides, you always knew you had a good chance of bumping into Elizabeth Taylor and Richard Burton in the elevator. (Our current entertainment media would have labeled the glamorous couple "Elizard" or "Richabeth.") Flying time back then was roughly a little over an hour and a half, not much more than today's flights.

While I traveled to New York frequently to participate in some of the agency's activities, my primary responsibility was to keep things moving in Cleveland. Lois was the driver of our Manhattan office. New York added Maidenform, *Family Circle* and Bed, Bath & Beyond. (Originally known as Bed & Bath, we suggested that they attach the "Beyond" to their name.

You like it better, yes?) Meanwhile, Cleveland grew substantially with Sherwin-Williams, TRW, British Petroleum, General Dynamics, Stouffer Hotels, and GE Lighting. However, both Jim Rucker and Steve Verba from our Cleveland strategic planning department were often active on New York office assignments.

Our New York office was featured in an article in *Madison Avenue* magazine in December of 1969. The reporter asked me if New York presented any different problems than we encountered in the Midwest. Here's what I told him: "In Cleveland, you get a guy sitting at a desk. He says, 'What we need is a syrup in a nice bottle that pours easy.' In six weeks, you've got a product and you're on your way. Here in Manhattan, things don't run that way, because between the guy with the idea and the guy who's doing the advertising, you've often got a lot of nervous people. There are so many layers to go through, they can slow down progress." Forty years later, I don't think that's changed. If anything, it's spread to the point of being a pervasive deterrent to efficient business operations.

Over the years, I enjoyed many wonderful and amazing experiences in New York. One of the most colorful, though, occurred on a trip that I unexpectedly ended up sharing with Carl Stokes. As most people know, Carl was the first black mayor to be elected to office in a major city in the U.S. The city, of course, was Cleveland. We got to know Carl, and he appointed us to handle his reelection in 1969, after having served an undistinguished two years. It was a close race against Republican Seth Taft, but Carl won by a very slight margin, 1,700 votes. We were euphoric.

We were crazy about Carl. Talk about charisma, he had it. Our creative director, Dave London, marveled at Carl's smile, personality, and ability to hypnotize an audience. He had a lot of celebrity endorsements as well. Jesse Jackson came to Cleveland to stump for his black brother. So did Bill Cosby. Bill told an almost all-white audience this story:

When I was in high school, I was third string running back on our football team. Over half the season was over, and I regularly bemoaned the fact that I had never gotten into a game. Why should the coach send me in? After all, he had All-City Goldberg as the starter and Jocko Deever, a fleet track star, as his second stringer.

It was the fourth quarter of a close game, and Goldberg was the victim of a vicious gang-tackle. They had to carry him off the field. Jocko went in for Goldberg, and suddenly I was next in line. The game raged on up and down the wet field. No team yielding; no team scoring. Suddenly, Jocko was hit in the backfield as his blockers got stuffed by a 200-pound lineman, and everybody piled on. Poor Jocko lay there stunned, with his uniform torn to shreds.

"Cosby!" the coached yelled. Wow! This was my chance. I jumped off the bench. "Cosby! Take off your jersey and give it to Jocko!"

I did. Jocko put on my clean, unblemished jersey. Sadly, I returned to the bench. But my jersey went around left end. My jersey dashed around right end. My jersey cut through the line for a big gain. Finally, my jersey scored a touchdown. We won the game. And, folks, Cosby smiled. Today, Carl Stokes is wearing my jersey.

Late one Sunday night, I boarded a plane bound for New York at Cleveland Hopkins International Airport. I wanted to get there in time for an early breakfast date at my favorite, the Regency Hotel. When I was getting off the plane at LaGuardia, someone tapped me on the shoulder. It was the Mayor, Carl Stokes. He was on the same flight, and we hadn't seen each other. We decided to share a cab into the city. He was there to get the Horatio Alger Award that day. We got in the cab, and I asked the driver to drop Carl off first at the Plaza on East 59th and Fifth and then take me to the Regency on 61st.

"No, no!" the driver indigently protested. "I go first to the Regency, then to Plaza." He had a thick Latin accent. I guessed that he was Puerto Rican.

"Look," I said, "Normally, you would do that, but his man is my guest, and I want to drop him off first. Understand?"

"No, no!" he screamed. With Carl and me sitting on the edge of the back seat as we tried to reason with him, he jammed his foot on the accelerator. We were jolted back against the rear of the cab and held on for dear life as the angry driver zoomed the cab out of the airport and sped recklessly and furiously onto the freeway, twisting through nighttime traffic, and finally screeching to a halt in front of the Regency. When he opened the rear door, he swore at Carl.

Carl was mad. He jumped out of the cab and grabbed the driver. Fists were flying. They wrestled to the ground in the gutter. Carl was definitely getting the better of it. I couldn't believe the scene. A stylish woman waiting for a cab in front of the hotel said, "Isn't that the mayor of Cleveland?"

"No. Of course not," I said, as I reached for Carl's suit jacket and pulled and pushed him into another cab. I put a $20 bill into the driver's hand and asked him to take Carl to the Plaza. We never discussed the event. It just happened.

I admired Carl. He had lifted himself from the city streets. He became a lawyer and was involved in several charitable organizations. He was urged to run for office by the business community and many liberal friends anxious to get minority representation in high places. He was very bright and well-informed. He spoke convincingly and passionately. He was movie-star handsome. He was ambitious for fame and success. His tastes for clothes, food, and women ran very high. However, he was a lousy mayor. He hated the discipline it took to run the city. He feuded with the City Council. He had problems with police chiefs. He despised the media who were quick to criticize him. Even many of his black friends felt that

Cal had abandoned them. Unlike his older brother, long-time and highly distinguished Congressman Louis Stokes, Carl was more suited to show business than politics.

At one point during his administration, Carl and I talked about his future and decided to do a pilot of a proposed Carl Stokes television talk show. We decided to tape it in New York City. Carl and I agreed on the first three guests. They were William F. Buckley, Jr., the conservative author and columnist; Reverend Jesse Jackson of Operation Push; and Meadowlark Lemon of the Harlem Globetrotters basketball team.

We went to Buckley's apartment and home office in Manhattan. It was charming and comfortable. There were lots of bookcases full of books and papers. Buckley's desk and typewriter were cluttered with magazines and newspapers. He had appointed his walls with numerous pictures in various frames. Many were scrawled with personal messages from the presidents, professors, authors and other famous people pictured. Buckley was friendly and soft-spoken. The interview with Carl had a funny twist. I felt that Buckley interviewed Carl more than Carl interviewed Buckley. But, this was Carl's first effort, and he quickly understood what he would have to do for the next guest.

We moved our cameras to a high school gymnasium on upper Lexington Avenue. Meadowlark Lemon, the affable clown prince of basketball, was already in uniform and shooting baskets. Both Carl and I put on sneakers and joined in the fun on the court. Carl was really good. I was pretty rusty and wondered what happened to the former John Adams High School Varsity player. Meadowlark and Carl sat in the stands near the sidelines. The interview went great. They were both very down to earth, relaxed, and funny. Carl was catching on fast. I could tell he had a future in this business.

The next day Jesse Jackson arrived from Chicago. We all had lunch first in a restaurant on East 59th near Madison Avenue. Everybody was cheerful despite the problems we had getting Jesse to show up for this interview. A few weeks earlier, I had gone to Chicago and sat through a Sunday Operation Push lecture meeting just to meet Jesse and his assistants, so that we could work out the arrangements.

At lunch in New York, Jesse noticed my Corum Gold Coin wristwatch. I love fine watches, own several of them, and this watch is one of my favorites. I'm wearing it right now. The highly skilled Swiss watchmaker scooped out an actual $20 gold piece and inserted the works of a precision watch. Then he strapped the exquisite timepiece with a genuine alligator leather band.

"I like your watch," said Jesse. "Let me wear it when we tape the interview."

"Really?" I responded.

"Sure," he said. "Let me wear it. I'll return it when we finish." Reluctantly, I gave him my treasured watch. He put it on his wrist and smiled at me. I felt a strange twinge.

The interview with Jesse was fairly interesting. We filmed the two old friends deep in a conversation as they strolled down East 59th Street. Our video cameras rolled backward down the street in front of them while they walked and talked. After it was over, there was a lot of jostling and hand shaking as Jesse settled into a long limo with his assistants.

"Wait a minute," I said, grabbing the limo door before they could close it. "Hey, Jesse, you got my watch."

"No," he said. "You gave me that watch."

"No way," I said. "I let you wear it, but it's my watch." He took it off his wrist and handed it to me. A Corum Gold Coin Watch is worth about $6,000. Even I am not that generous.

I showed the finished "Conversations with Carl Stokes" pilot to several TV station program directors. Nobody bought it. They all had suggestions on how to do it better. After his mayoral term ended, Carl was snapped up by WNBC-TV in New York to anchor their key news show. So, something good came out of it after all.

My previous little excursion into Manhattan with Carl marked Wyse's first venture into political advertising. Thankfully, it turned out to be our last.

Marc (standing far left) and the Smucker's staff promoting jellies, jams and the funny-named product that had to be good on WJR radio.

With Mayor Ralph Perk at his side, Marc addresses a press conference at Cleveland City Hall.

Marc sharing a laugh with his assistant in his office at Wyse Advertising.

Marc (seated front right) and staff preparing for a pitch. Music, singing, and some innovative ad concepts made the pitch anything but dry and boring.

Marc and Art Director David Spreng discuss a campaign, circa 1965.

Marc (left) turns his well-trained ear to ponder the sound at a recording session in the mid-1960s.

Marc (left) apparently likes what he's just heard, while talking with an unidentified man, Eve Reisz and Adeline Gasparelli.

Seated at the head of the table at Thomas', a Greek restaurant on the main floor of the 2800 Euclid Avenue building, Marc celebrates a great client win with some of the Wyse Advertising staff.

Marc and Lois Wyse listen to the vocalist sing a jingle in a recording session.

Marc (right) tucks into a delicious dinner at one of the many company clam bakes, living the Wyse Advertising motto: Work hard, play hard, and have fun at both.

Marc and Paul Smucker accept one of the hundreds of awards they won for outstanding marketing and advertising campaigns.

Awards night at the Cleveland Society for Communicating Arts. (L to R) Lisa Hughes, copywriter; Donna Solpa, broadcast producer; Dave London, creative director; Marc Wyse; Chuck Withrow, copywriter; Gary Pilla, art director; Mike Marino, associate creative director and writer; Dan Fauver, art director.

The time clock in the 2800 Euclid lobby was never functional, but it really wasn't needed. People couldn't wait to get to the Wyse offices. The place was rockin' on a daily basis!

WYSE ADVERTISING
**Marc A. Wyse**
Chairman
25 Prospect West • Cleveland, Ohio 44115
**216-696-4045** Fax 216-736-4425
E-Mail: mwyse@wyseadv.com
www.wyseadv.com

Marc's business card was a little piece of paper loaded with a lot of power to open doors, win friends, and influence businesses.

During a housewarming party at the Landmark Towers Complex, Marc gives a tour of the new offices to John Morikis (left) and CEO Chris Connor (right) of client Sherwin-Williams Stores.

The many faces of Marc Wyse, entrepreneur and CEO.

Taking his own advice, Marc had the idea to buy poster space at Cleveland Hopkins International Airport so that clients and potential clients would get the Wyse Advertising message coming or going. The firm produced a new one every year.

Another example of an airport poster. These were also
formatted for print ads in advertising trade magazines.

Yet another example of an airport poster. These were also
formatted for print ads in advertising trade magazines.

# 9 | Roll On, Big-O!

Alliteration has somehow always been an amusing, if only a coincidental part, of Wyse Advertising's business history. We had four major clients whose names began with the letter "S" — Sherwin-Williams, Smucker's, Seagrams and Stouffer's. At one time, we had three clients headquartered in three cities with almost pronunciation-defying names. They were Coshocton, Ohio (GE Textolite); Cochecton, New York (The Catskills Visitors Bureau); and Conshohocken, Pennsylvania (Lee Tire).

We also had two client CEOs, one in the '60s and another in the late '80s and early '90s, that had significantly similar names and significantly similar fates. One is William Howlett, former chairman of Consolidated Foods (now called Sara Lee), and the other is William Hulett, the president of Stouffer Hotels.

This is a story about our experience with the former, William Howlett. In the early 1950s, Howlett had served as president of Nesco Inc., a manufacturer of housewares. He resigned in 1952 to become general manager of O-Cel-O division of General Mills Inc. before becoming president of the Lawson Milk Division of Consolidated Foods. I first met Howlett when he was running the Lawson Milk Company of Cuyahoga Falls, Ohio. Lawson's was a chain of 700 convenience food stores throughout Ohio. Howlett, a bright, innovative marketer, was assigned the Lawson Milk division after the parent company, Consolidated Foods of Chicago, bought the business from the Lawson family. My timing was almost perfect. Four months after I had first contacted their ad manager, Ralph Brown, Howlett had become unhappy with McCann Erickson, so several agencies were asked to contact them.

When I met Bill, I immediately felt I had a friend. He was a short man with a happy, cherubic face that glowed with ideas and searched out people who could keep pace with him. He faced the challenge of tying all his stores together with a central theme. Ralph Brown's art department did the retail newspaper ads. They were looking for an agency that was strategic and could do great radio and television creatively. For our presentation, we had a song demo recorded in a New York studio by a very professional group.

Our copy theme line was simple and to the point: "Aren't you glad you live near Lawson's?"

Howlett loved it, and we got the account. Or as Ralph Brown called to say, "You win the weenie."

In this business, you learn a lot from smart clients. Howlett asked me to attend brainstorming meetings in his office every Tuesday at 8 a.m. It was almost an hour drive from my home to Cuyahoga Falls, so often on frigid winter mornings I would leave home when it was dark outside. On arrival, there would always be a large cup of Lawson's Orange Juice poured out of their glass jugs awaiting my cold hands and dry throat. Howlett would smack his lips and say, "You know, this orange juice is fresh-squeezed, and 40 hours ago these oranges were picked in Florida. The oranges were squeezed, and the juice was rushed to us by tank trucks. We bottled the juice and shipped it to our stores, all of this in a matter of 40 hours."

Thus was born the legend of "The Big-O." We rolled it out in the form of a television commercial that we filmed on a highway in North Carolina. [I recently found it on YouTube under "Lawson's Big-O Orange Juice Commercial (1970s)".] The commercial showed a shiny steel tank truck wheeling down the road over bridges, through tunnels, over hills. There were two drivers because it was nonstop. Our Frankie Laine-style ballad hammered home the exciting story:

"The Ballad of the Big-O"

[Spoken] This is the story of a tank truck express they call "The Big-O." She hauls Lawson's fresh-squeezed orange juice nonstop from Florida.

[Sung] Roll on Big-O,
Get that juice up to Lawson's
In 40 hours.

Now the oranges ripen in the Florida sun,
Sweet on the tree they stay.
Then they pick 'em and they squeeze
Just as quick as you please,
And the Big-O leaves the same day.

Roll on Big-O,
Get that juice up to Lawson's
In 40 hours.

Now one man sleeps
While the other man drives
On the nonstop Lawson run,
And the cold, cold juice
In the tank truck caboose
Stays as fresh as the Florida sun.

Roll on Big-O,
Get that juice up to Lawson's
In 40 hours.
Get that juice up to Lawson's in 40 hours.
Get that juice up to Lawson's in 40 hours. [Fade]

Lawson's "Big-O" orange juice became a remarkable success. The Florida Citrus Commission called to find out what was going on in Ohio. Lawson's broke every sales record they ever had. I give Bill Howlett full credit for coming up with this idea. Wyse creative people merely fine-tuned it. The catchy tune is still considered by many, especially anyone born before 1960 in Northeast Ohio, to be one of the most memorable advertising jingles ever.

Howlett was a big idea man. Of course, not all of his ideas were practical. At one point, he wanted to fly in fresh sweet corn from South America in January. Howlett's background, I later learned, had been in the PR business. He knew how to create events. During World War II, he had worked for Carl Byoir, the prestigious PR firm. One of its accounts was Willys Overland Motors, which manufactured the famous military utility vehicle. According to Howlett's brother, David, the name "Jeep" had been used as a nickname by a soldier who took the name from Eugene the Jeep, a strange animal with mysterious abilities in the *Popeye* comic strip. "But it was not identified with the vehicle," David added. "Bill made the connection and christened it."

He had an appealing enthusiasm for challenge, and a big one came his way. Ohio's Blue Laws (antiquated but still on the books) regulated Lawson's right to stay open on Sunday. The large supermarket operators in the state had all agreed to save labor costs and stay closed on Sundays and evenings. They regarded Lawson's 700 stores as a threat and put pressure on the legal system to enforce these laws. After a prolonged debate and hours of legal battles, it was decided to put the problem before Ohio's voters. A statewide referendum on the Blue Laws ("Keep 'em or kill 'em.") was on the ballot. Howlett was ready for the most stimulating campaign of his career.

No prospective Ohio Governor or Senator ever did a better job of campaigning than Bill Howlett. He toured every county and every corner of the state. He spoke at rallies, clubs, and churches. He spoke and debated on radio and television. He gave Wyse a "whatever it takes" budget to buy ads in newspapers, radio and television throughout the state. This was the most exciting political slugfest we'd seen in a long while. I was even involved in it. The opposition identified themselves with the amorphous name of Retail Merchants Association. They were well-funded by supermarkets and department store operators. They spent a lot of money on media, but they lacked one thing — a candidate like Bill Howlett. Howlett won by a big margin. Ohio citizens got what they always wanted: stores open when they wanted to shop.

Howlett was definitely a winner for Consolidated Foods. They acknowledged that when they transferred him to head up Sara Lee Bakeries, their fast-expanding frozen baked goods division in Deerfield, Illinois. Soon he became chairman and CEO of the huge company itself, until he resigned in 1969 and then became chairman of Ward Foods Inc. until he retired in 1977. He died in 1986.

While he was chairman of Consolidated Foods, I called him one day when I was in Chicago. He insisted that we go to Wrigley Field the next day to see the Cubs play. We each munched on hot dogs as we tanned in the warm, sunny stands, watching the Cubs lose to the Cincinnati Reds. The only thing missing was a nice, tall glass of chilled Big-O orange juice.

# 10 | The '80s: Decade of Change

My decade of the '80s started with a major change: Lois and I got divorced. She had grown more committed to New York than to me or Cleveland. But we remained business partners in this exceptional little agency we had started and grown into a major player in the industry. I served as chairman and head of the Cleveland office, and she became president and ran the New York office. We had 90 people working in Cleveland and 30 in New York.

Wyse Advertising had certainly come a long way from the cramped, one-window office we once shared with an artist in the Carnegie Hall Building at 1220 Huron Road, near Public Square. In 1981, we relocated our offices to some pretty nifty quarters on the 17$^{th}$ (top) floor of Stouffer's Hotel, which was one our big clients. We even had our own private elevator that whisked people to and from our elegant lobby with Oriental rugs and potted plants. I had long ago replaced the sawhorses and boards I had used as my first desk with a delicately detailed, antique English desk that now holds a prominent place in our home library. I never had doors on my office, either. So, it was always open to anyone who needed to see me. If you have meetings and things going on behind closed doors, people always think there's something secret going on.

We had, however, become famous for one particular design feature of our décor. By the 1980s, I had amassed a significant collection of Alphonse Mucha posters. Each time we received a package that an art dealer shipped to us, we had them flattened, framed, and hung throughout our offices. We also had a beautiful assortment of antiques appointing every nook and corner, all complemented by gorgeous oriental rugs on the hardwood floors. I believed in providing a richly decorated office to foster the creativity of our staff who devised the powerful campaigns that by then had long been the hallmark of Wyse Advertising.

But among the antique toys and trucks and trains, the Tiffany lamps and natural and stained wooden furnishings, exposed brick, vases with flowers, old books and miniature bumper cars, vintage radios and phonographs, and even some classic penny arcade games, those Mucha posters were my favorite. I had started collecting them after I first eyed some of his intricately illustrated posters that were the crème de la crème of 19<sup>th</sup> century European advertising.

A Czech born in the remote Moravian town of Ivancice in 1860, Mucha grew up to become the most fashionable decorative artist of Belle Époque Paris. By the 1890s, at the height of his fame, his style was characterized by beautiful women drawn with long, flowing hair and sweeping, sensuous lines. He was also known for his exotic flower motifs typically drawn in subtle, muted pastels. His impact was so significant that architects and craftsmen would integrate his style into their building and furniture designs. He was probably best known, however, for his *panneaux* (signs) *decoratifs* and posters for the theater, including one he designed for the famed French actress Sarah Bernhardt.

I used to read as much as possible, whatever I could get my hands on, about Mucha and posters and poster collecting. In June of 1985, I came across an article in *Art Business News* that claimed that American poster collectors numbered more than 10,000, according to a *Business Week* study. The article went on to quote an international poster-collecting expert who said that while most collectors wanted to know how many copies of their posters exist, no one really knew, because they weren't created as art to be carefully hung in galleries or chateaus, but as advertisements to be "slapped up on walls" on street corners and in alleys. The highest demand, the article added, was for posters by Toulouse-Lautrec, A.M. Cassandre, Jules Cheret, and our adopted favorite, Alphonse Mucha. I understood and studied the value of our posters, but really I just loved the superb colors, the luxurious lines, and the wonderful whimsy of these antique, Art Nouveau advertisements.

In 1980, we made an acquisition of a different kind: the Sapin & Tolle advertising agency, which was best known for its major industrial client, TRW Inc., a Cleveland-based Fortune 500 company that was a long-time leader in the automotive, aircraft and aerospace technology industries. Throughout the years, we crafted a number of award-winning print, radio, and television ads for TRW. I'm proudest, though, of our groundbreaking computer animation TV spots that were created long before the Pixar era. According to our writer, Chuck Withrow, who now lives in Columbus, Ohio, these commercials were unlike anything else that you saw on television at that time. The first of these innovative spots brought to life a tribute to surrealist artist M.C. Escher's birds and fish, and the tagline was, "Just when you think you see the whole picture, the picture changes." The suggestion was that TRW provided the pioneering technology required in the fast-evolving, high-tech world for clients to "see" the current demands and develop the appropriate solutions for their customers.

Several years later, I landed one of my best hires. I had a met a young man, Howard Landau, in Washington, D.C., at an event. He was working in the public relations industry at the time, while his wife, Ellen, an art professor and Jackson Pollack and Lee Krasner expert, was working at The Corcoran Gallery of Art and The Smithsonian. In 1982, they moved to Cleveland so that Ellen could take a teaching position at Case Western Reserve University. Howard called me, looking for work. We had a spirited and informative discussion, but as he says, I was an advertising man, and I just wasn't ready to venture into public relations, so he took a great job at National City Bank. Wyse was the advertising agency for NCB, so Howard and I occasionally ran into each other, even though he wasn't managing advertising for the bank.

A year or so later, my son, Rob, developed a business plan for a Wyse public relations division. He and Howard met for lunch to discuss the plan and so Rob could obtain his response and recommendations. Howard thought it was well-conceived and written and with a thorough market analysis. He was quite surprised, however, when I called him the next day and asked him to join us to help launch the new division. Rob served as president and Howard vice-president of Wyse Public Relations.

That was 1984. By then Wyse had grown into Cleveland's largest ad agency, with 174 employees. We needed more space, so we did something else no one was expecting — a tactic we had grown quite proficient at employing — when we suggested building a bridge across a back alley of West Huron Road to connect the 17th floor of the hotel to the 15th floor of the Terminal Tower. By walking down a short flight of steps, you'd be in the Terminal Tower, and we moved the growing Wyse PR offices into that new space.

While I had earmarked Howard to have one of the most spectacular offices in Cleveland, with fabulous views of Public Square and downtown, I also gave him one of his scariest publicity assignments ever. I showed him the drawings and told him that we had to meet with the City Council and Architectural Review Board to get their approval for the bridge construction project, so there was probably going to be some press. He imagined an editorial cartoon in *The Plain Dealer* the next day showing a bunch of bridges connecting to the Terminal, saying "Wyse Desecrates Historic Terminal Tower." It all worked out fine, though. We got the approval, and everyone loved the project because we were a growing business in Cleveland. The bridge is still there. You can see it from behind the Terminal Tower, if you're standing near the Old Main Post Office building that was built in 1934 and is now known as M.K. Ferguson Plaza.

Still, things didn't work out exactly as we had originally hoped for Wyse Public Relations. We had thought the new wing could provide public relations services to our major clients such as Sherwin-Williams, Smucker's, and Stouffer's Hotels. While our name and reputation did help open doors for these potential clients, at the start the division was operated solely by Rob and Howard. So, those prospects politely declined, knowing that two people couldn't possibly run effective PR campaigns for companies of their size and reach. Besides, they already retained large firms, usually in New York, to handle their PR.

When the dream of providing services across the entire marketing platform didn't materialize, Rob and Howard went out and pounded the streets to hustle their own clients. They were very aggressive and did a great job building an impressive client list. Soon, though, Rob moved to New York to help Lois in our office there, so Howard began to build the business on his own, hiring people and winning new accounts. One day, he came to me and suggested that we rebrand the company, since he was competing against renowned public relations firms, and Wyse was known for advertising. I suggested that we call it Wyse Landau PR, and of course, over the next decade, Howard continued to grow the division into one of the premier public relations businesses in the industry.

He told me recently that he always appreciated the way we ran our divisions, including market research and direct marketing, with the bottom line as the incentive for the managers to perform well. By doing so, we encouraged entrepreneurism, since the division heads would run each division as if it were a separate company and become successful on their own. "I never even knew I was an entrepreneur until you brought that out in me," Howard said. He also felt that I always had a good eye for recruiting people who became personally invested in the business as if it were their own and could manage Wyse's accounts properly, serving as good counselors to their clients, providing great service, and doing it profitably for the company.

As a self-made man, I have always believed in and supported entrepreneurship. We always fostered a collaborative culture within Wyse, too, where there wasn't much backbiting or politics, but instead everyone worked together — and had fun together — for a common cause. That certainly helped us keep clients in the event that an account manager, say, or an art director left the company. But more important, it made for a much more happy, effective, and creative office. I recently spoke to Jim Rucker, who ran our Smucker's account team for about 25 years and retired as our vice chairman in January of 2001. He reminded me how the advertising industry standard for staff longevity was approximately 2½ years, while Wyse Advertising's average length of employment was closer to ten years, and we had many people who stayed for 20 years or more.

There was another change in the '80s that wasn't so good. In 1988, my brother Jack died. He had launched and run his beloved *Properties* magazine for 42 years. The memorial issue that was published in December of 1988, shortly after his death, featured a thick tribute section with a beautiful love letter from his wife, Beatrice, and articles from his daughter Norita, who wrote about "the gentle man of quiet dignity, unstudied elegance and quintessential warmth" who was her Dad, and several close friends, including Sam Miller, philanthropist and co-chairman of Forest City Enterprises, which now owns Tower City Center, formerly known as the Terminal Tower, and uses our old space on the 15th floor as part of their headquarters.

I wrote a piece that was entitled "My Guide, My Teacher, My Advisor and My Coach" to reflect all of the contributions he had made to my life. I don't think I could write anything more appropriate about him now, so the following is the text of the article:

My big brother Jack was my guide, my teacher, my advisor, and my coach for over 60 years. Hardly a day went by that he didn't find time to talk to his "little brudder."

As a young kid, I was known as Jack's tail. Our parents insisted that I accompany him on his dates. After all, we couldn't afford babysitters.

As a handsome teenager, Jack had a passion to be well-dressed. He had an especially keen eye for high-fashion neckties. His vast collection of ties astounded his depression-poor friends. Little did they know the neckties actually belonged to our Uncle Arthur, who lived in our house.

Jack frequently borrowed Uncle Arthur's ties. He neglected, however, to tell Arthur about the borrowings, and this became a great matter of turmoil in our house, especially when soup stains and wrinkles began appearing on brand-new neckwear that our Uncle Arthur had purchased, but never worn.

Jack won a Paul Whiteman [an American bandleader and orchestral director] singing contest. And at the age of 18, he decided to seek his fortune in Chicago, because a friend had given him the unused part of a round-trip railroad ticket to Chicago. My tearful parents and I went to the railroad station to see him off. We waited and waited. The train never showed up. We had gone to the wrong station. Jack never went to Chicago. Aren't we all thankful for that. Just think how all of us would have missed the happy times we shared with Jack.

I recently came across a letter I had written to Jack on August 25, 1942, when I was 19. "Dear Jack," I started. "This is something I've owed you for a long time. It started away back about nine years ago when I was ten years old. You remember me then, Jack, a tall awkward kid, with wild, unkempt hair and a flying shirttail. I was quite large for my age even though I hadn't as yet had the feel of a pair of long pants."

I went on to tell him how I had watched him go through a "fine transformation" into a man and how I had never thought of him as anything more than just an older brother, until he took me under his wing and "took real pleasure in helping me grow up." I recalled our Friday night and Sunday morning basketball games that helped us get truly acquainted. Then I reminded him of how, when I got to junior high and received my first "calamitous report card," he rescued me and taught me how to study and concentrate.

I closed the letter by saying: "Someday, I feel that we'll do great things, you and I, whether we do them together or just help each other along. I hope that even with your increasing responsibility of a wonderful growing family we can always maintain this same harmonious relationship." We did, and we did.

Fortunately, many other good and delightful things happened during that decade. Do you want to know the absolute best thing about the '80s? (And then the '90s and '00s.) I met my beautiful wife Sheila on a blind date. I had been dating a variety of women and having a lot of fun while doing so. Some, I'll have you know, even considered me one of Cleveland's most eligible bachelors. Howard Landau still kids me about how I learned to bake pies so that I could bring my favorite, a lemon pie, to give my date upon arrival as a gift. "You always find a way to be creative," he said.

Then, in 1982, a mutual friend told each of us about the other. So, one day I was sitting in my office, and I called Sheila, who ran her own, highly successful beauty salon business, and said, "Why don't we meet for fifteen minutes, have a drink, and just see if we like each other? Then I have to go to my art class. I'll meet you after work in the lobby of the Stouffer Hotel on Monday, October 27." She said, "I don't know who you are." I said I would be carrying an artist's portfolio case that I used for the drawing classes that I sometimes took at The Cleveland Institute of Art. Back then, we couldn't Google each other's image or biography on our iPhones. "We discovered each other the natural way," Sheila says.

So I came down from our Wyse offices, walked into the lobby, and saw three women sitting on a long bench. I approached the first one, and I said, "Sheila?" She said, "Sheila?" She shook her head. "Oh, thank God," I thought. I went to the next gal, and I said, "Sheila?" She said, "No." Then I saw this lovely woman, and I said, "Sheila? Oh, my God!" Something told me this was right.

"Have you had dinner?" I inquired.

"What about your art class," she countered.

"What art class? Let's have dinner."

We finished our drinks, and we went out for supper at Pier W. That night I thought to myself: "This is the woman I am meant to be with. She's gorgeous. She owns my heart already. She's going to be my soul mate."

At one point during dinner, Sheila asked, "Do you have a job?" She had already been married, too, and wasn't going to suffer any fool who wasn't gainfully employed. "Yes, I have a job," I assured her. We dated for a while, and I didn't miss any of those other girls at all. I never did go back to that art class, either. We got married on May 22, 1983. Those fifteen minutes turned into 30 years. We've been together ever since that blind date. We still have the bench. Bill Hulett gave it us when Stouffer's remodeled their lobby years later.

For a long time, we lived in huge, magnificent home in Hunting Valley, where I swam laps in our pool every day. I love to swim and have almost always had a pool in my back yard, ever since I dug that first, ill-fated mud hole on East 154th Street! Now, we have a comfortable and beautifully decorated penthouse apartment behind Beachwood Place in The Hamptons. It's just wonderful. Appropriately, our building complex offers two swimming pools, one indoor and one outdoor, that I take advantage of as much as possible. There's a fantastic Italian restaurant,

Tuscany, downstairs that we love, and we're close to many other great amenities and restaurants, including one of our all-time favorites, Jack's Deli and Restaurant on Cedar Road. Fittingly for this chapter, they were founded in 1980 by Alvie Markowitz, his brother Harry, and their father Jack. We eat there almost every Tuesday, so that we can enjoy their corned beef and cabbage special.

I have to tell you, though, I'll never forget that moment when I was in the hospital after my stroke in 2005 (More on that later.), and Sheila said, "We sold our house." I said, "You sold our house? Where do we live now?" She had found our gracious loft on top of a building, and we enjoy it very, very much. We put three places together, so that we would have more room as well as a cozy, pleasant, and private place for our delightful daughter, Jennifer, when she comes home from New York.

Now, each day I can admire our Alphonse Mucha posters, artworks, antique toys, cars, trucks and trains in every room and can still enjoy a panoramic view outside. I guess I have a thing for elegantly appointed penthouses.

As for those Mucha posters, many of them remained in the Wyse offices after we sold the company. (More on that later, too.) But we now have many of the posters prominently displayed throughout our home. I must have done something right as a collector. We recently had a meeting with a curator from the Cleveland Museum of Art, one of the finest in the country, and they have asked us to consider donating our collection.

# 11 | Creativity Wins!

Actually, we had some big ups and downs in the next couple of decades, too. That's what makes business — and life — interesting. If you're not ready to ride the roller-coaster that is business, don't get on the ride. In 1990, Wyse Advertising was named one of the 30 "hottest" agencies in the country, having recorded billings of $140 million the previous year, as we closed out the '80s with a bang. A year later, though, in January of 1991, we had to reduce our workforce by about 10 percent, due to weak conditions in our industry.

A few years later, in 1994, we lost the main Smucker Company account to the Leo Burnett Company in Chicago, one of the top ten ad agencies in the world. The primary reason was Smucker's dominated the U.S. market by then, so they saw their future growth happening overseas, and Burnett offered substantial international advertising capability. Around that time, I heard an anecdote that Smucker's Goober peanut butter and grape jelly product had become extremely popular in Asia. Perhaps the company saw this as a sign. We did continue to do some smaller projects for them, however, whenever Tim or Richard needed us.

As a result of losing the Smucker's account, we could no longer sustain a full-service agency in New York, so we had to close the shop. Lois, who was running a publishing business by that time, did continue a Wyse presence there, and we occasionally used her offices for new business pitches. Despite all of the downturns, our Cleveland office remained healthy, and we were able to keep 185 people working hard at being creative. We could also boast American Greetings Corp., BP America, BF Goodrich, and Stroh Brewery among our clientele. By 1995, we were hovering near the $140 million in annual billings mark, too, so the Wyse ad machine was humming along nicely. Our long list of high-profile clients included Applebee's International and Renaissance Hotels International, whose parent company, New World Development Company of Hong Kong, had acquired our client Stouffer Hotels and Resorts from Nestlé in 1993 and folded it into the Renaissance chain. For the former, we developed the tag: "Applebee's, America's favorite neighbor. You belong at Applebee's." They operated roughly 1,000 restaurants in 48 states and six foreign countries, and their advertising expenditures totaled $35.5 million in 1998, which was significantly up from approximately $28 million in 1997.

Truth is we had grown so much by 1996 that we needed a lot more space. We explored several options. Should we move into a smaller building downtown that we could call The Wyse Building? Should we build our own building? We had big dreams and big ideas. We had a broker working for us, and we looked at a lot of spaces, mostly in the heart of Cleveland where we belonged.

Not long before our search began, LTV Steel Corp. had declared bankruptcy, as the steel industry continued to wrestle with foreign competition and ongoing decline in the industry. (LTV ceased operations in December 2001 and sold its production facilities to an outside group of investors, International Steel Group, in February 2002.) The timing was bad for them and great for us, as their spectacular headquarters space in the Republic Building became available. A group of us took a tour and immediately fell in love with the space. It had that warm, distinctive ambiance with a lot of wood and brick that we preferred, plus it had a rooftop deck like we had in the hotel. It was in the heart of the city and across the street from where we were. We could just picture ourselves there, since it just felt like Wyse. We negotiated a favorable deal. We took over four floors and 50,000 square feet of the building, one of three that comprise the Landmark Office Tower at 45 West Prospect Avenue directly behind the Terminal Tower.

We were ecstatic to relocate once again our extensive collections and antique appointments that enhanced our playful office setting. Many of our employees worked at intricately carved desks and solid 19th century pedestal tables in offices that they decorated with their own toys and treasures, such as model airplanes, gumball machines, a framed butterfly collection, and even an Elvis "swivel hips" clock. We had kitchenettes on each floor, so that people had access to full-size refrigerators, coffeemakers, microwaves, vending machines, and breakfast bar seating. We even had a cappuccino machine, and one of our conference areas had a foosball table and another a putting green so that our employees could unwind when they needed to, clear their minds, and maybe ruminate on a few creative ideas.

When visitors exited the glass elevator into our new lobby, they were greeted by a resplendent bird of paradise plant and a towering grandfather clock. The piece de resistance, though, was our lunchroom. Rather than shove it into some back hallway, we dedicated a commanding corner of our glass-enclosed top floor. We loaded it with amenities, too, from a 27-inch television and VCR to a pinball machine and jukebox – all of which were overshadowed by the floor-to-ceiling windows that framed panoramic views of Gund Arena, Jacobs Field (now Quicken Loans Arena and Progressive Field) and a stretch of the torturously twisting and turning Cuyahoga River.

Our staff-accessible rooftop deck with benches and tables proffered a birds-eye view of Public Square and Cleveland's downtown skyline. There, our folks could relax in wrought-iron chairs or on wooden benches around the perimeter and gaze at the Lake Erie shoreline. Sheila used to kid me and ask, "Why can't we just live here?" But I wanted to make it inspiring, and our people thoroughly enjoyed working in our playful and unconventional atmosphere. They deserved it. So did I.

The second half of the '90s certainly held its share of turbulence for Wyse Advertising. In 1996, we ended our 30-year relationship with Stouffer Hotels or at that point, Renaissance Hotels International. We added Dayton-based Mead Products to the fold. We also regained a former big-name client when we took on the Sherwin-Williams Store account. Then we acquired Cleveland's six-year-old Blasko, Sipos, & Courtney agency, adding its $3 million in annual billings to Wyse's $140 million. In 1997, we landed one of our largest new clients, the $30 million national advertising account for Office Depot. The good news was that we secured the rights to employ Scott Adams's popular Dilbert comic strip character for an extremely popular campaign, the first time Adams had scripted his cartoon for television commercials. The ads touted Office Max as the official school supplier of the National PTA. The bad news was we lost the account a year later.

Sometimes you may lose an account, and it is definitely not your fault. That's how I felt in 1999, when we lost Applebee's. We had worked not only with the management of Applebee's, but with the individual franchisees in the different markets, so that was a lot of people to keep happy. I recall the day that the president of Applebee's said that they were lucky that we were their agency. Still, I have to be honest. I don't think we provided our most extraordinary work for Applebee's. One thing we did right was find a great food photographer from New York who made their entrées look extremely appetizing. I believe that if you are advertising a restaurant client's cuisine, make people feel that they absolutely must have that particular food. They should practically be able to taste these delicacies when they see them on the TV screen or view a print ad.

At one point in the '90s I had a bit of a strange experience. Walmart ran an ad in newspapers around the country. The ad featured a photograph that was very familiar to me: a picture of a big rocking chair that we had used in some of our General Dynamics ads. I called the company in Bentonville, Arkansas, to tell them about the copycat ad. I also made an off-hand remark to the gentleman that I spoke with that I had just purchased a pair of shoes at a Walmart store for $4; I said I couldn't believe it. I usually paid as much as $20 for the same pair at other stores. He apologized for including that picture in their ad, which had been created by his agency in Kansas City. The ad, which was done for a holiday campaign, was pulled. A week later, he sent me another pair of shoes, just to thank me.

In 1996, in recognition of all the fantastic work he had done to build our PR division, I set up a new legal arrangement with Howard Landau to create a new company that was a 50/50 partnership between Howard and me. I had always treated him that way anyway, but this made it official: Howard was no longer an employee; he was an owner. In 1999, we worked out another deal, and Howard became the 100 percent, sole owner of Landau Public Relations. A year or so later, he found his own space in the Warehouse District and relocated there. It was just time for him to move on and take complete control of his company, and I supported his growth and success entirely.

For all the bumps and jumps in the '90s, the last year of the decade did see us prove our mettle — and one of my mottoes "Creativity wins!" — when we gained widespread recognition for our Sherwin-Williams national advertising campaign, with the now-famous slogan: "Ask how, Ask now, Ask Sherwin-Williams." Founded in Cleveland by Henry Sherwin and Edward Williams in 1866, The Sherwin-Williams Company has not only grown to be the largest producer of paints and coatings in the United States, but was then and remains now among the largest producers in the world. The company had been a Wyse client in the '80s, until they went with another agency for several years. They then spread their ads for different divisions among a few agencies.

In 1998, Sherwin-Williams moved creative responsibilities for its Paint Stores Group, a $30 million–$40 million account, back to Wyse Advertising in Cleveland from J. Walter Thompson, which had handled the account from its Detroit office since 1995. That win was especially meaningful for us because it reunited our agency with one of our major accounts that we had handled in the 1980s. We also liked working with Cleveland-based companies. Moreover, we had created the "Ask Sherwin-Williams" tagline that the company has used ever since and continues to use today. The top corner of their corporate website reads: "Ask Sherwin-Williams. No matter where you are in the world or what surfaces you're coating, Sherwin-Williams provides innovative solutions that ensure your success."

At the time, Sherwin-Williams operated more than 6,000 retail stores in the United States. (Today, they have around 3,900 stores.) Their competitors became the increasingly popular "big box" stores such as Home Depot and Lowe's that catered to people wanting to improve their homes. Sherwin-Williams' competitive edge is that each store has a manager who was very familiar with how to use paint and what paint to use for a particular job. We believed the "Ask Sherwin-Williams" theme underscored the competitive edge that Sherwin-Williams had over the big box outlets.

The slogan was a collaborative effort; we worked together to develop the tag line. We were interviewed by David Fuente, who was president of Sherwin-Williams at the time. He said that he wanted to meet our creative director, our account executive, and me to see how we all got along. We had an informal meeting in my office. He hired us on the spot. David London, a veteran at Wyse, was our creative director at the time. He had started as an art director, and ended up working closely with Lois and me on many of the Wyse agency's winning campaigns. David L. had a lot of experience, especially with retailers, including Higbee's department store. David F., on the other hand, after a couple of years, left Sherwin-Williams and became the president of Office Depot, with a headquarters in Del Ray Beach, Florida.

We ran commercials on national television in several spot markets. At that time, the company also took on several fashion lines, such as Ralph Lauren Paint and then Martha Stewart. They have reached a fashion-conscious female audience. However, their brand paints are exclusively sold at Sherwin-Williams stores.

It is important to find out what customers a client isn't reaching, so that you can look for more opportunities for sales. I thought there was a better way to reach a female audience. Housewives were often frustrated because they may have a background in art or design, and some women are just great decorators. They knew their color needs, but they didn't know what products to purchase. I thought we could attract some of these women to work at our store. I told Chris Connor, and he wanted to implement the idea in their various stores. I recommended that Sherwin-Williams talk to Ikea, a tremendous Swedish company that makes furniture at a very good price point that could be put together by people at home. He was very excited. Most people in retail agree that Ikea has done a superb job in reaching young people who have limited budgets but great taste. These customers should be advised by trained decorating and painting experts who are stationed in their stores. While big box stores continue to be popular, they have not been totally successful in selling paint, since they have failed in employing trained professionals to help consumers with their décor.

Recognizing the increasing demand for their unique line of products and services through their stores, Sherwin-Williams asked us to create a new store advertising campaign that we rolled out in the first quarter of 1999. At the time, Bob Wells, who was the director of marketing for the Stores Division, wanted to place more emphasis on stores rather than individual products. "We want to focus on the Sherwin-Williams store as the solution for consumers' decorating needs," he said in an article in *ADWEEK*. "I don't think we've given enough attention to the store itself in past advertising, but that hasn't been the fault of our agencies. We've always acknowledged the importance of the stores, but we as a corporation have not focused on that as we should have."

Bob also told the trade publication that while they recognized that the growth of home centers had brought new competitors into the market, the change in advertising focus was not a response but an acknowledgement of the competitive advantage Sherwin-Williams had with its stores. The year before the paint giant returned the work to our shop, the Stores Division had spent $32 million on advertising.

One of the smart hires I did not make was Chris Connor, who went on to become CEO of Sherwin-Williams, where he continues to lead the company to bigger and bigger successes. After Chris graduated from Ohio State University in 1978, he came to Cleveland to begin a career in advertising. He applied to every single advertising agency in Cleveland, starting with Wyse, and others throughout Ohio. I can honestly say I don't even remember interviewing him or what he was looking for then. Looking back, I probably did him a favor. He once joked that he counts among his most prized possessions the Wyse Advertising rejection letter he received informing him that he "wasn't going to cut muster at this great shop." He was hired by Meldrum & Fewsmith Advertising in Cleveland and assigned to the Glidden Paint account. Glidden is another industry-leading paint company that was founded in Cleveland in 1875 by Francis Harrington Glidden and Levi Brackett as a varnish-maker.

Eventually, Sherwin-Williams hired Chris as the Director of Advertising — just as Wyse secured the account in 1982. They informed him of this during his interview, and they showed him the television ad we had just completed during which a man cannot find his favorite striped couch because his wife just had the room painted in matching stripes. The tagline is, "Next time, you'd better Ask Sherwin-Williams."

"There I was thinking to myself, 'This is my chance,'" Chris recalled at a luncheon a few years ago. "These guys would not hire me out of college. I am going to shoot this agency right in the foot! Then I see this great campaign. 'Ask Sherwin-Williams.' So simple. So crisp. So perfect. And here we are some years later still under the tagline of 'Ask Sherwin-Williams.'"

At one time, Chris was the head of Special Products at Sherwin-Williams (Minwax) based in Solon. He was a natural to take over as head of the company. He is a wonderful man to work for and with because he is very open and enthusiastic about the business. Chris is also very innovative. He got the idea of creating a new kind of paint can. He went to a product design company Nottingham-Spirk, two very creative guys in Cleveland who also developed the spinning toothbrush. They developed a plastic can for Sherwin-Williams that is lighter and more convenient to carry and features a lip that makes it easy to clean your paintbrush after re-applying paint to the brush. Sherwin-Williams ran many ads introducing this new can in both nationally televised spots designed by Wyse and in the trade publications.

With our "Ask Sherwin-Williams" campaign, Chris believes that we had captured the essence of what it meant to shop at the company's specialty paint store chain that offers advice and high-quality products, a reputation that has stuck with Sherwin-Williams through all of these decades. He believes that it helped the company grow dramatically, from a one- or two-billion-dollar business to one with annual sales in the $8 billion range. During their tenure with Wyse, the company added more than 1,500 stores. Beyond the business, Chris and I became close friends. I always love talking to him whenever we see each other. We shared many a meal. He was more of a breakfast guy, but he knew I was more of a lunch guy, so he humored me, and we had numerous wonderful lunches. We both loved to work, so we did discuss the fun things in life, but 95 percent of the time, we were moving forward our ideas of how things could be even better. That's why Chris credits us with more than 20 years of nurturing their brand to make them the preeminent leader in paints worldwide.

In the late '90s, we won the account back through dogged determination, but we also did what we did best for them: We became a vital part of their company and contributed as much as we could to make them better at advertising their amazing products and store services. I was deeply touched and found it quite fulfilling when Chris said the following at that same luncheon in 2006:

"In your life, you get a chance to meet giants, the men and women who lift you up, who help you become more than you ever thought you could be, who provide you shoulders to stand on, and Marc has been that kind of man. He's been a trusted business advisor, a counselor. He has come up with an untold number of ideas. One or two of them actually good! But nevertheless, always ideas. Always, always challenging us to think about ways to improve this company and this brand."

One of my favorite stories from that decade involved me giving a simple but significant idea to someone famous worldwide. Bill Gates to be exact. On March 3, 1998, *Time* magazine threw a giant 75th Anniversary for their Persons of the Year cover boys and girls at Radio City Music Hall in New York. We did a lot of advertising with *Time,* so our names were added to the guest list that included global superstars Muhammad Ali, F. Lee Bailey, Bill Clinton, Joe DiMaggio, Mikhail S. Gorbachev, Lee Iacocca, Evander Holyfield, John F. Kennedy Jr., Henry Kissinger and Martha Stewart, as well as Hollywood wonders Mel Brooks, Tom Cruise, Kevin Costner, Tom Hanks, Sophia Loren, Stephen Spielberg, and Sharon Stone.

At one point, I found myself chatting with Microsoft Corp. chairman and personal computer guru Gates. He was very pleasant. Then, indicating the Coke-bottle specs in horned rim frames that he favored, I said, "Bill, why don't you get rid of those glasses?" He was a bit stunned. "They make you look like a nerd. While you're in New York, why don't you go out and get yourself some new glasses?"

He turned to his wife, Melinda, and said: "Did you hear what this guy just told me?"

"Well, he's right," she replied.

I never spoke to him again, but I'm pretty sure he had been told the same thing by others closer to him than I was. The next time I saw him on television, I noticed he was sporting far more stylish spectacles than he had at that megagala. Hey, by then I had been in this business for 50 years, so I certainly wasn't shy about dispensing sound marketing advice to anyone, whether or not you were a billionaire, computer genius on the cover of *Time*.

# 12 | Savoring the Glass Apple

When I left my own company, I didn't get a gold watch. I got something much better. At a tribute luncheon that I will tell you more about in a minute, Tim and Richard Smucker presented me with a stunning Stueben Glass apple that their father Paul had displayed on his office desk for many years. Now, it sparkles on my desk in our library. I see it every day. Elegant in its simplicity, the Steuben's Apple has remained one of the famed glassmaker's most versatile and popular gifts since 1940, when they first produced artist Angus McDougall's iconic design. For me, it serves as a constant reminder of Paul, the highest ethics possible in business, and the infinite fond memories I have of our years working with the Smucker family and their company.

Understanding and emphasizing the highest ethics and moral standards are important, because I know people often think of advertising as a cutthroat industry, especially in light of this recent cable TV show, "Madmen," that I absolutely hate. Our agency and our approach to advertising were the diametric opposite of this imaginary, rather sordid television firm. We always worked hard to be the best salesmen for our clients that we could be. Our perspective was if they were successful, we were successful. We always worked with the greatest, highest-quality clients, too. For instance, Smucker's has been on the prestigious *Fortune* list of the top 100 places to work since its inception in 1998, and Sherwin-Williams makes the list on a regular basis.

Advertising alone does not make a product succeed. It was important that we researched the ultimate consumer to learn their preferences and what they look for specifically in each client's products or services. At Wyse, we tried to dig deeper on the wants, needs, and preferences of the people we were trying to sell. Our simple creative philosophy remained the same throughout the years: There shall be a good takeaway line with the client's name in it. A lot of advertising today just isn't as effective, because ten minutes after you see it, you can't remember whom it was intended to promote. It's great to be entertaining, but not at the client's expense.

At Wyse Advertising, we were always interested in being part of a successful sales story. Our personality was to become partners with our clients. We wanted to know the bad news as well as the good news. What a client could or couldn't do. We liked a close, confidential relationship. We were almost always part of our client's strategy team. We helped make judgments and recommendations that assisted in client growth and profit. In a productive agency/client relationship, it should be difficult to tell the agency from the client. We did not provide "yes" men. Instead, Wyse could be abrasive, critical, and daring. We thought that open communications was part of our job in helping improve our clients' businesses.

I once read an article in *The New York Times* that talked about practical intelligence being an executive's greatest asset. I implemented my practical intelligence by hiring the best people I possibly could find to make our business strong and make me look good. Advertising is exciting because agencies engage with a lot of different companies. Advertising professionals are involved with new trends, new ideas, and new lifestyles. The people in our business must spot these trends, and be able to ride the waves that follow. That's why we needed good, sensible people who could sort out the facts, make good decisions, and then collaborate with other people to get the job done. I always looked for people with the following qualities: passion for business, a creative spirit, a confident personality and sense of self-worth, ambition and a commitment to growth, and last but far from least, ethics. Additionally, I calculated that an intelligent, young person could learn everything they needed to know about our business in roughly six months.

Getting back to that first hiring requirement, I have always lived life for the joy that's in it. I loved our business. I never felt like I was "going to work." I believed it was a challenge every day, and I love a challenge. To succeed in advertising, you must have a passion for it. You must love it. And I did. Just walking in the door each day and seeing all the new, good creative stuff we were generating excited me tremendously.

Also, I would be lying if I didn't admit to the exorbitant amount of fun I had while doing my job. Heck, I got to dance with Ginger Rogers in my office once when she was visiting to appear at a benefit for the Cleveland Play House when I was a member of the Board. I had just moved into my new office, and a friend of mine who was proud of how we had decorated our offices was giving her a tour of Wyse. I was standing at my desk, and I said to her just on a whim, "Hey, Ginger. May I have a dance with you?" She said, "Sure." So we danced a little bit. Not to music. She was so pretty, and she smelled good. She stayed about half an hour. The next day, there was a picture in *The Plain Dealer*. I talked with her a little bit. What do you say to a film dance legend? But now I can say I danced with Ginger Rogers.

Although I wasn't the greatest duffer ever to hit the links, I also got to play a round with golf legend Arnold Palmer at a special event to advertise a Palmer-designed golf course near Pittsburgh. I had a beat-up old putter, but as golfers often do, he wanted to see it — and then he ended up keeping it! Of course, over the years, Sheila, Jennifer and I, along with many of our friends, have enjoyed spending time in our gorgeous getaway, winter home in Providenciales in the Turks and Caicos Islands, which are a British Overseas Territory.

If I have one decade I didn't enjoy as much, it would be this last one. In October of 2004, when I was 81, I still served as chief executive of Wyse

Advertising; we had offices in Cleveland and Detroit, and our agency counted DaimlerChrysler AG, FirstEnergy, Medical Mutual Insurance Co., Moen, PolyOne Corp., Rockwell Automation, Royal Appliance Manufacturing Co. (for whom we had created the eye-catching "We suck" advertising campaign), Sherwin-Williams, Timken Co., and the University Hospitals Health System among our clients. We had annual billing of $115 million and employed 100 in the Cleveland Office. Not bad, considering that after 9/11, advertising budgets were cut all across the country, and the industry had yet to totally recover from that tragedy.

Still, even at my age and after more than 50 years in the business, I worked full days and came in on weekends. Yes, I also still thrived on the thrill of the chase for new business and big, high-profile clients. I got just as fired up helping our long-term clients continue to succeed and get all the attention they deserved. In a profile Janet Cho, a seasoned business reporter, wrote about me in *The Plain Dealer* on October 5, 2004, she quoted Chris Connor: "Here's a guy who should be resting on his laurels, enjoying his retirement down in Florida," my old friend said. "Instead, he's up here in Cleveland, on a cold February morning, sticking his finger in my chest, telling me how I can sell more paint. I love that."

Obviously, my index finger was fine, and even though I had a slight tremor and tendonitis in my right thumb, I swam 40 to 50 laps a day in our pool at our Hunting Valley home. I would make the rounds of the agency two or three times a day, just to see what everyone was working on and throw in my two cents now and then. I was still brimming with ideas, and I never minded if people thought some of them seemed wacky. That's how it is with creativity. You generate a lot of ideas. Some will work. Some won't. Overall, I was at the top of the world.

One year later, however, my perspective dropped a few levels. The difference? I had a stroke in October of 2005 and had to retire from daily operations at Wyse. I also had to undergo extensive rehabilitation. The good news was, almost exactly a year later, in September of 2006, I was the guest of honor at a tribute luncheon at Windows on the River in the Flats District of Cleveland overlooking the Cuyahoga River, similar to the majestic views from my office. At the luncheon, I looked out over the more than 300 family members, longtime friends and business colleagues from a wheelchair. Organized by Sheila and Jennifer in coordination with the Cleveland Advertising Association, the event raised more than $15,000 toward the Marc Wyse Advertising Scholarship we had established for Ohio students studying communications. I had always enjoyed counseling young people who were interested in the business, so the opportunity to give them a hand financially just made sense.

My old friend and former employee Norm Wain did a phenomenal job as master of ceremonies, with beautiful Cantor Sarah Sager providing a touching invocation. Many of my good friends spoke, including Chris Connor, chairman and CEO of Sherwin-Williams; Bill Hulett, retired chairman of Stouffer Hotel Co.; Richard Smucker with his brother and fellow co-CEO Tim in the audience; and Tom Embrescia, president of Second Generation Ltd. Tom, one of my few friends taller than me — though now everyone is taller than me, since I find myself mostly sitting down — was a hoot as he took off his suit jacket and launched into his customized rendition of "My Guy" with the help of several audience members. At an early age, Tom had gotten his start selling radio time, and then went on to acquire several radio and TV stations in the U.S. Today, he is the best media salesman I have ever met, mostly because he knows exactly what to put on the air to attract the appropriate audience.

When Richard Smucker spoke, he awarded me the glass apple "retirement gift" that I treasure today. He said: "Marc, as a symbol of how our business began with apple butter, which was our first product, my father always had a Steuben apple on his desk, and as a small appreciation for our friendship and what you've done for the Smucker Company, we want to present to you that Steuben apple."

Later, my lovely and amazing daughter Jennifer, on her way to completing her degree at Barnard College, gave a marvelous speech about her old dad, and then introduced me. With the help of Sheila, who has supported me in countless ways for the past three decades and now held my right side, and my trusty attendant, Otis Bailey, who is several inches taller than me, held my greatly weakened left side, I managed to tell some fun and funny stories about my life and business career for 45 minutes. I got a lot of laughs, but the biggest was when I told the story of how my father, Leib Zisha Anshelovitz, was forced to change his name to Louis Weiss when he and my mother arrived at Ellis Island. "Can you imagine the name 'Anshelovitz Advertising?'" I quipped.

That luncheon is one of the few fond memories I have since my stroke. After it happened, I traded full days at the office for eight-hour days at Euclid Hospital's outpatient physical therapy department. I had tried several other programs, but the spirit of the people working there was wonderful. Trying to learn to walk again, make my left side understand that it has to move, trying to get my brain and muscles to coordinate was one of the biggest challenges of my entire life. And I did say I loved a challenge, didn't I? I guess I never could set aside the advertising part of my brain, though. At one point, when we were doing our daily trek up and down the halls, with my left leg strapped to the right leg of Kevin Daykin, my occupational therapist, I turned to him and said, "You've got something very special here. You've got to sell it." Kevin just smiled and said, "Good job, Marc. Are you ready to stop?" "No," I replied. "Let's go just a little farther."

For additional support, I also used a brightly spangled walking stick that I affectionately named "LeBron" because it was tall, strong and didn't let me down. Well, that affection dissipated somewhat after LeBron left the Cleveland Cavaliers and took his talents south. One the one hand, you can't dismiss his abundant and extraordinary athletic gifts, but as public relations go, he really dropped the ball with how he handled that strategic move to Miami.

Once my therapy progressed to a point where I could function reasonably well, I did start going into the office a few days a week. However, by 2006, Lois, who had been diagnosed with cancer, and I decided we needed to sell the agency. We had a strong management team in place to ensure that our company survived long after we left. We had several offers, but in the end, we chose to sell 90 percent ownership of the company to four of our employees who had been quietly managing the agency during the previous few years anyway. Neither of us was in shape to run Wyse Advertising anymore, and we wanted to resolve the lingering uncertainty about our firm's future.

Our timing was good. The deal was official in January of 2007, and Lois died not long after that in July. But our mighty little agency continues on to this day under the same name we started with back in 1951: Wyse Advertising.

Looking back on more than 60 years of exceptional, award-winning and business-building creative campaigns, I am exceedingly proud of the Wyse Advertising legacy within the industry nationally as well as in the world of Cleveland business. I can tell you from the bottom of my heart, the Kinsman Cowboy has never forgotten where he came from, nor have I ever taken for granted all of the amazing family, friends, and business colleagues who have shared and enriched my life — especially Sheila and Jennifer.

I've often felt like I've lived five or six different lives, and each was more fruitful than the last. I had the opportunity to enjoy my work and my personal experiences, a chance to challenge myself continually, and keep growing as a man, a husband, father and grandfather, and as a businessman. Even after the stroke, I said, "Okay, this is my new life, my new challenge; I'll do the best I can to beat it." If there is one lesson I have learned, it's that life's a lot more enjoyable when you face each day with a positive frame of mind. So, I can honestly claim, if I had my life to do all over again, I wouldn't change a thing. I've enjoyed every minute to the fullest.

As I write this, I am reminded of a great book that I have owned for many years, an anthology of poems by Robert Frost. After studying with him while he was poet-in-residence at Dartmouth, I can say he was one of the finest writing teachers I ever had. These days, it is difficult for me to hold down the pages of a book. We tried all kinds of devices, but the most effective was a simple rubber band that now keeps the book open to my favorite poem of his, "The Road Not Taken." These are the closing lines:

Two roads diverged in a wood, and I –
I took the one less traveled by,
And that has made all the difference.

I love that poem, and I have often referenced it, because we all face crossroads at different times. If we're fortunate, we make the right decisions and move forward. If we take the wrong path, then we have to keep the memories, good or bad, move forward with determination, and try harder the next time.

My point is no matter what life throws at us, we must never give up. We must embrace the struggles and the exasperating moments as much as we celebrate the victories and the exhilarating moments. When you have a chance to choose the road not taken, don't be afraid to take it. I did. It made all the difference.

# ACKNOWLEDGEMENTS

Marc was a "Wyse" guy and an extraordinary man. We were fortunate to share our lives together for almost three decades.

Marc entrusted us with the awesome responsibility of spreading his wisdom through completing the publication of his book. It encapsulated, in Marc's voice, the story of his life and career. He was a "guru" of advertising.

Marc was a man respected and revered for his unique creativity and determination. A classic man of dignity, he was truly considered a legend in his time — even now — posthumously.

As I write this today, October 27, 2012, it was 32 years ago today that we met on a blind date. "Let's meet for 15 minutes and see if we like one another." I guess we did.

A very special and heartfelt thanks to Marc's longtime friends and colleagues, Dan Fauver and Howard Landau. Without their guidance, expertise and perseverance, this project would not have come to fruition. Thanks to them and so many others for their love and support in getting Marc's book published. The alphabetical list follows. And I so hope I haven't left anyone out. Thank you all from the bottom of my heart.

And thank you, Marc, for this honor.

Love, always,

Sheila

**Dan Fauver**, longtime Art Director, Vice President and Associate Creative Director, Wyse Advertising. Now works from an office at Melamed Riley Advertising on PlayhouseSquare, Cleveland. DanFauver.com, DanFauver@ me.com

**Margaret Ann Gibson**, the amazing personal assistant everyone should have. Thank you for your patience and computer skills as you listened to Marc and captured his thoughts in print, and for always going above and beyond.

**Jerry Hoegner**, former Vice President of Account Services, Wyse Advertising; then Vice President of Sales Promotion at The May Company; then Senior Vice President of Sales Promotion at Higbee's Department Stores; then Director of Marketing Services at *The Cleveland Plain Dealer*. Now retired.

**John Jefferson**, former Account Supervisor, Wyse Advertising. Has been operating Jefferson & Assoc. since 1990. jjefferson.com, adman@jjefferson. com

**Christopher Johnston**, the wonderful writer who worked with Marc so relentlessly to achieve his voice, organize and express what was important to Marc as he reflected on his life. ChristopherJohnstonWriter.com

**Berenice Kleiman**, longtime friend and the one who was able to condense Marc's thoughts and feelings so succinctly on the Dedication page.

**Howard Landau**, President, Landau Public Relations, longtime friend and business associate. Howard was instrumental in helping us find Chris Johnston, the writer with the best fit to Marc's personality. hlandau@ landaupr.com

**Martin Reuben & TRG Reality**, has and continues to execute many brilliant visuals for the Wyse art directors. Contributed once again with photos of the book for publicity. trgreality.com

**Jim Rucker**, Vice Chairman, Wyse Advertising. Now retired and traveling the world with his wife, Gene.

**Peter Winzig**, Vice President, Account Supervisor, Wyse Advertising. Now Director of Marketing & Corporate Development at Weltman Weinberg & Reese, LPA. pwinzig@weltman.com, weltman.com

**Chuck Withrow**, longtime friend, Writer and Creative Director, Wyse Advertising. Retired to a boat on a landlocked lake with his lovely wife, Mary Kay. Refuses to wear socks.

**Jennifer B. Wyse**, our loving daughter, whose Introduction to Marc's book is both thoughtful and beautifully written. She is a terrific young woman who has made both Marc and me proud.

| # Wyse Advertising
# All-Time Client Roster

**(As of December 2011)**

Adelphia Cable
Akron Cablevision
Alside Aluminum
American Express — Travel Service Division
American Greetings
Angostura Bitters
Applebee's Restaurants
Arhaus Furniture
AT&T

Bed Bath & Beyond
Benesch, Friedlander Attorneys
BF Goodrich
Blue Cross Blue Shield
Bonnie Bell Cosmetics
British Cunard Line (*Queen Elizabeth II*)
British Petroleum
The Buffalo Sabers

Caritas Hospitals
Carl Stokes for Mayor

Carlton Cards
Carrier Transicold
The Catskills
Cavanaugh's Steakhouse
CBS Radio Network
Clairol — Herbal Essence Shampoo, Clairesse
The Cleveland Browns
The Cleveland Cavaliers
Cleveland Center for Economic Education
The Cleveland Clinic
The Cleveland Indians
The Cleveland Press
Climalene Company (Bowlene, Linco Beach)
Club Aluminum
Cole National
Consolidated Natural Gas
        The East Ohio Gas Company
        Hope Gas Company — West Virginia
        Peoples Gas Company — PittsburghRiver Gas Company
        West Ohio Gas Company

DaimlerChrysler AG
        Freightliner Trucks
        Sterling Trucks
        Western Star Trucks
Del Laboratories: Sally Hansen Hard As Nails

East End Rambler

First National Bank
First National Supermarkets
        Edward's Food Warehouse
        Finast
        Pick-n-Pay

First Seneca Bank
FirstEnergy
Fisher Cheese
Fisher Foods
      Fazio's Supermarkets
      JAX Deep Discount Stores

Galatin Bank
General Dynamics
General Electric Batteries
General Electric Lighting Business Group
General Electric Textolite
Genie Garage DoorsGoodyear Tire & Rubber
Grabski Motors

The Higbee Company
Honey Baked Ham
Hoover
Hyatt Hotels and Resorts

Inn Maid Noodles
Integra Bank

The J.M. Smucker Company
      Preserves, Jams & Jellies
      Ice Cream Toppings
      Frozen Pies
      Pickles
      Majic Shell
      Mary Ellen
      Dickinson's
The Joseph E. Seagram Company

Kellogg Cereal
Kelly Services
Kendall Oil Company
Keybank

Lampl Fashions
The Lawson Milk Company
Leaseway Transportation
Lee Tire and Rubber Company
Lender's Bagels
Longchamp's Restaurants
Lyon Tailors

Maidenform
Manners Big Boy Restaurants
Marathon Oil Company
McDonald & Company Securities
Medical Mutual Insurance Co.
Michigan Fruit Canners — Thank You Brand Pudding & Pie Filling
Mid-Continent Telephone Company
Mr. Coffee
Mr. Gasket
Moen Faucets
        Stanadyne, DIY Faucets

National City Bank
The New York Yankees

Office Depot
Old Times Ale

Pacific Crest Investment Bank
Penny Brite (copper cleaner)
Penton Publishing (*IndustryWeek*)

Piaget Watches
Picker
PolyOne Corp.
Preview Subscription Television (Division of Time, Inc.)

RAX Roast Beef
Rayco
RCI
Renaissance Hotels & Resorts
Revlon — Milk Plus 6
Rockwell Automation
Royal Appliance Mfg. (Dirt Devil Vacuum)

Scripps-Howard Broadcasting
Sealy Mattress
The Sherwin-Williams Company
      Retail Stores
      Martha Stewart Paint
      Martin Senour Paint
      Pratt & Lambert Paint
      Ralph Lauren Paint
      Super KemTone Paint
      Williamsburg Paint
Siematic Kitchens
Sterling Jewelers
Sterns & Foster Mattress
Stouffer Hotels & Resorts
Stouffer Restaurants
      Cheese Cellar
      Eden Glen
      James Tavern
      John Q's
      One Nation
      Pier W

Roxy Bar & Grille
Rusty Scupper
Top of the Town
Stouffer's Frozen Foods
Stouffer's Ice Cream
The Stroh Brewery Company
    Augsburger
    Goebel
    Piels
    Schlitz
Sugardale Foods
Swiss Industries Group
Swiss National Tourist Office

Tappan Air Conditioning
Tappan Appliances
Thisledown
Thompson Electronics (Indy Office acct)
Ticor Tile
Timken
Toast of the Town Hosiery
TransOhio Savings Bank
TruTemper
TRW

United Jewish Appeal
United Way
University Hospitals Health Systems

Vitamaster Exercise Equipment
VitaMix

Waccamaw Pottery (Homeplace)
Wendy's Restaurants

Westfield Insurance
White Farm Equipment
WCBS-TV
WKYC-TV
Woodhill Chemical
      Duro
      Permatex
      Super Glue
WWWE Radio

# The Wyse Guys:
# All-Time Employee Roster

(**As of December 2011***)

Marc Wyse
Lois Wyse
Kathy Wyse
Rob Wyse

**Cleveland Office**

Pat Agee-Dobro
Jan Ainsworth-Harcourt
Sylvia Albertelli-Masek
Carmen Alcorn
Denis Aleksander
Ed Alexander
Bob Amer
Debbie Amodeo
Christy Anderson
Jennifer Anderson
Lorraine Anderson-Bivin
Susan Anderson

---

* Apologies to anyone we may have unintentionally excluded.

George Andrews
Matt Arko
Alicia Arnold

Donna Baltas
Sharon Bando
Cherie Banks Meyers
Maria Bardossy
Lynn Baucco
Jeffrey Bauer
Becky Bearden
Denise Beck
George Becker
Edward Bedock
Casey Belcon
Debi Belt
Michelle Berry
Don Berwald
Krista Beyer
Betsy Biggar
Denice Bjurman-Tichy
Len Blasko
Diana Blunk
Laura Bobrowski
Anita Boczek
Jim Bodziony
Chuck Boggs
Michelle Bollman-Kosir
Bethany Borger
Jeffery Borger
Chuck Borghese
Michael Boyd
Ro Breehl
Casey Brennan-McGannon

Susanne Brockman
Nancy Brown
Sandy Brown
Charlene Bruno
Robert Bruosta
Tracy Burke
John Butler
R. J. "Buz" Buzogany

Kelly Cairns
Ernie Caldwell
Roberta Calcagni
Bob Calmer
Vicki Calvin
Carl Camden
Ron Campana
Chris Campbell
Marlene Cardona
Patricia Carey
Jennifer Carlson-Toms
Joe Carlton
Kevin Carmont
Jim Carroll
Judy Carroll-Lavrich
Linda Cathcart
Mark Cerame
Anna Chanakas
Michael Chaney
Julie Charvat
Courtney Cherna
Lisa Christensen
MaryAnn Citraro
Annette Coffee
Natalie Colabianchi

Maryanne Cole
Mary Conway-Sullivan
Bill Cooper
Anita Cosgrove
David Courtney
Elizabeth Covington
Jeff Cox
JoAnn Crowder
Mark Crowley
Dick Croy
Nancy Culura
Mike Cunningham
Ron Curilla

Darla Dackiewicz
Jody Dana
Steve Daniel
Frannie Danzinger
Bill Davis
Jennifer Davis
Larry DeAngelis
Joanne Deas
Antoinette (Toni) DeJohn
Brandon Delia
Lou Dell
Sal DeMarco
Judi Demmerle-Smith
Lydia Demidow
Errol Dengler
Brooke Denney
Beth Dessoffy
Tammy Detrich
David Diehl
Laura Diorio

Ken Dobro
Judy Dolata
Richard Dolesh
Denise Dragin-Wyse
Roz Drenik-Stevens
Mike "Doc" Dreyfuss
Sharon Dziak

Marie Eatough
Jennifer Eden
Don Effler
Carol Eichman
Carol Eisenberg
Lauren Embrescia
Gail Eovito
Mort Epstein
Darlene Ewolski-Porter

Dan Fauver
Holly Fazio
Laura Fejzoski
Vince Felber
Erik Fenberg
Meredith Ferguson
Pat Ferlin
Keri Fetzer
Don Fibich
Dan Fields
Aylie Fifer
Denise Fike-Albertino
Patty Fintak
Dee Fludine
Judy Flynn
Candy Forest

Suzanne Fortunato
Peggy Finucan
Lenny Flontek
Matthew Forbes
Dwayne Freed
Jeremy Freeman
Jack Fristoe
Jill Fristoe
Mike Fruchey
Jeanmarie Fucci
Bob Fulton

Linda Gable
Kathy Gabrosek-Walters
Jim Gagen
Linda Galdun
Jeannie Gampietro
Cheri Gardiner
Shawn Garber
Bill Gardner
Adeline Gasparelli
Janet Gaydosh
Patty Gelin-Velotta
Bill Glubiak
Bob Gold
Marsha Goldberg
Edwina Gough
Mark Graf
Marci Granlund
Pam Grealis
Matt Greene
Phil Greene
Jeanine Grega-Delsanter
Ted Grigg

Ryan Groff
Lori Gross
Neil Guiliano
Elaine Gustafson
Susan Gutierrez
Ronnie Gutin

Clete Haas
Susan Haas
Irene Hajduk-Devine
Mark Hamer
Susan Hanlon
Derek Hannah
Joe Hannum
Mike Hardman
Amy Harris
Kathy Harris
Kirsten Harris
Linda Harris
Marshall Harris
Steve Haught
Bob Haverback
Tracey Hayburn
Patty Hayes
Fred Haynes
Dave Hazelbeck
Lou Heckman
Jim Heilman
Annette Heinbach
Karen Heise
Lisa Hendershot-Fauver
Eva Hendricks
Vivian Henoch
Sandi Hensel

Julie Herceg
Dave Hibbard
Wendy Hiendlmeyer
Sharyn Hinman
Pete Hlinka
Samantha Hodges
Jerry Hoegner
Greg Hoeth
Baron Hoffer
Joanne Hoglund
Sharon Hohnen
Sandy Homes
Dinah Howey
Elizabeth Hudgings
Denny Hudock
Karen Hudock
John Hughes
Terry Hughes
Jim Hunt
Chris Hunter
Anita Huntley
Heather Hurd
Joan Hyatt
Therese Hyland

Leah Imler
Saul Isler
Denise Ivan

Christine Jackobs
Sue James
Dave Jankowski
Norma Jankowski
Jackie Janowski

Ginny Janusz
Debbie Jarab
Jackie Jasko
John Jefferson
Michael Johnston
Lynn Jonela
Katherine Jouriles

Joel Karabinus
Georgia Karides
Karen Kariotakis
Cindy Karklin
Dan Karp
Cindy Kaserman-Podway
Susan Katz
J Kellon
Sue Kempton
Francie Kennedy
Katrina Kenyon
Susan Kidd-Dailey
Lisa Kieffer-Hughes
John Killpack
Kelly Kishbaugh
Carolyn Kmieck
Heidi Koch
Eric (Rick) Koehler
Jan Kovach
Hutson Kovanda
Lisa Kowalski
John Kozsey
Lynn Kramer
Betsy Krantz
Craig Krejci
Tina Kresic

Joan Kriikku
Kathy Kroeger
Matthew Krupa
George Kubas
Barbara Kuppersmith
John Kushera
Holly Kutina
Rick Kuttler
Bob Kwait

Steve Lageson
Marc Lance
Howard Landau
Stephanie Landes
George Lang
Patrick Langdon
Jenifer Lansky-Walsh
Dave Lauderback
Emily Lauer
Jean Laurianti
Jim Lawrence
Dan Leary
Lorraine Lee
Pauline Leidy
Ellen Leighty-Mishaga
Marybeth Lemon-Basten
Susanne Leone
Jim LeSueur
Jordan Levy
Tom Liebhardt
Meredith Linamen
John Lisko
Ann London
Dave London

Paul Lorko
Joan Lowe
Dave Lowery
Wilard Lunte

Lisa Mackey-McLean
Kathleen Mackin
Bob Malko
Michael Manelski
Sandy Manfrey
Diane Manuelli
John Marefka
Mike Marino
Betty Marks-Brown
Howard Marks
Maggie Martin
Michael Martin
Wendy Marquardt
Katherine Marusic
Dennis Matz
Kim McBee
Erin McCarthy
Kevin McCarty
Doug McClatchy
Patrick McGill
Christy McMillan
Mike McMullen
Cathy McPhillips
Roberta McNellis
Susan Meek
Terry Merecicky
Frannie Mervis
Todd Mesek
Joe Messinger

Bob Mickey
Kathleen Mickey-Cusatis
Barbara Miller
Pat Miller
Sandy Millman
Jim Monastra
Reggie Mooney
Mary Moorman-Gagen
Jim Morey
Jan Motter
Cookie Moyer
Maura Mueller
Yvonne Mulak
Michelle Mulchin
Jeff Mundson
Mary Sue Murphy
Sharon Mushahwar-Pinchot

John Naegele
Dave Nehamkin
Diane Neiderman
Jay Nelson
Brian Nemeth
Tom Nipper
Jeff Nomina
Laura Norman
Joe Norris
Gayle Novak

Karen O'Brien
Kathy O'Connell
Tom O'Connell
Tom Okal
Sally Olds

Larry O'Neil
Steve Orkin
Tom O'Toole
Jacie Otlowski-Schultz
Laura Owen-Yoder

Denise Palagyi
Fran Palasak
Toni Palese
Paula Pappas
Tracey Parker-Bentler
Mike Pastelyak
Sue Patterson
Connie Paul
Rebecca (Becky) Paumier
Ken Perdue
Lou Perlaky
Jorie Perry
Gary Peterman
Anya Peterson
Mary Peterson
Karen Pfaff
Sue Pflasterer
Gerry Phillips
Joe Pianecki
Wally Piasik
Gary Pilla
Lesley Pildner
Mary Ann Pirro
Gloria Piscura
Jim Pockmire
Brian Pokorny
Wendy Poltorek
Tom Pope

Kathy Posey

Jim Postma

Lisa Previte

Marcie Primrose

Jennifer Proudfoot

Nancy Prusa-Spinos

Mary Puissegur

Dave Pullar

Sharon Pullar

Lisa Randazzo-Feder

Ed Rapport

Larry "Moose" Rassmussen

Bob Rath

Eve Reisz

Chuck Repetti

Kathleen Richardson-Crosby

Carol Richmond

Bob Riley

Denise Rini

Susan Robinson

Wendy Rodman

Beth Ross-Yurich

Scott Rothmann

Carolyn Rowles

Rob Roy

Jim Rucker

Carol Rumjack

Ann Russo

Julie Ruszinski

Jerry Rymont

Jon Sakola

Jeff Salkin

Laura Salvatore-Calmer
Nancy Samanich
George Sapin
Marie Scalia
John Schaaf
David Schiever
Teri Schneider
Alan Schuessler
Diane Schuster
Celeste Sciortino
Terry Scott
Kate Seavers
Kimberly Sebastiano
David Sebold
Jen Sedlecky
Rick Seich
Linda Sellers-Bremkamp
Adam Sembrat
Alberta Shanley
Sarah Shatila
Mary Ann Shea
Jane Sherwin
Barb Sievers
Phil Sipos
Dean Skinner
Marilyn Smayda
Don Smetna
Bill Smith
Jeff Smith
Leslie Smith
Mike Smith
Tom Smith
Peggy Smolik
Celia Solloway

Chuck Solly
Brian Soloski
Donna Solpa
Paul Spencer
Donna Spies
Les Spizak
Dave Spreng
Patty Stachowicz
Bob Stam
Sue Stanovic
Chris Statzer-Murphy
Jan Staub
Pat Stawicki
Scott Stawicki
Steve Stawicki
Sharon Stieber
Julie Ann Stolzer
Sally Stone
Lesley Storme
Roseanne Strelka-Lowe
Suzanne Stelman
Lane Strauss
Westley Stump
Jack Suvak
Mark Szczepanik

Bobby Taylor
Julie Telesz
Helen Thomas
Anne Thomason
Todd Thompson
Amy Thonnings
John Thorne
Pat Tiburski

Terry Tichy
Mary Ann Tipple
Laurie Tischler
Jan Tittle
Amy Tix
Jerry Tolle
Michelle Tomsic
Ned Tookman
Karen Toorish
Bill Trausch
John Trivelli
Bill Troy
Barb Tsivitse
Christian Turner
Wendy Turner
Scot Tyler

Cindy Uhas

Carla Valentine
Kim Vallar
Dorothy Van de Motter
Rich Van Overberg
Steve Verba
Chris Viola
George Vlosich
Kendra Vogel
Keith Voracek
Jan Vulku

Cindy Wagner
Kenneth Wagner
Norman Wain
Rob Waldheger

Barbara Walker
Jan Walker
Anne Walters-Scott
Diana Ward
Cynthia Wargo
Gerri Webb
Kaley Weiss
Maggie Weitzel
Leslie Welch
Bob West
Ed Weszlowski
Eric Wheeler
Ollie White
Tim Wild
Dana Williams
Elizabeth Williams
Gayle Wilson
Joe Winklemann
Amy Winn
Mitch Winnick
Pete Winzig
Andrea Wisniewski
Chuck Withrow
Edna Wohlgemuth
Cathy Wolf
Lyn Wolfson
Jude Woods
Kathy Wright

Kristin Yamani
Rob Young
Steve Yuan

Cheryl Zajac
Debby Zanglin
Pat Zarak
Dave Zebroski
Jennifer Zeff
Pat Zivich
Howard Zoss
Amanda Zwick-Chandler
Melissa Zygaldo

**New York Office**

Karen Asmanis

Marilyn Baines
Joanne Barbieri
Maggie Bixler-Foster
John Bobbi
Gary Boens
Angela Bou
Diane Burton

Paul Cappiello
Maria Coletta
Phil Congo
Mary Alice Corbett
Irene Corrigan
Kathy Crafts

Anne Dempsey
Patricia Doherty

Michael Ende

Nancy Feldman
Peggy Fitchwell
Sarah Fleming
Barry Frey

Nat Gayster
Aviva Gordon
Georgia Graham-Love
Cindy Greenfield
Bob Grossman

Meegan Hanrahan
Pamela Hartford
Barbara Higgins
Paul Howard

Melody Izen

Susan Jablonski
Bobbi John
Lisa Johnson
Mark Johnson

Kathy Keesee
Ed Keller
Tom Kirmeyer
Lynn Kost
Dale Kramer

Sara Leadholm
Ruth Lebo
Joy Leckrone
Bob Lennox
Carolyn Lewis
John Lippman

Jane Maas
Holly Mahla
Cliff Marrero
Judith Mayer
Patti McCarthy (NY & Cle)

Carole Nugent

John O'Brien
Dina Olstad-Rice

Peter Pappas
Lynn Paster
Mary Pearsall
Roz Pellitier
Ann Peterson
Martha Pfeffer

Kathy Reyes
Eileen Riordan
Sarah Rogers
Anne Rudden
Pat Rutz

Gene Samuelson
Allan Saperstein
Leah Sapezone-Cetera
Renata Schaller
Bridget Schiotis
Lisa Sepalla
Charlie Sforza
Mary Ann Shea
John Shima
Linda Stillman
Linda Strauss

Rose Tibaldi
Lorraine Todd

Vicki Van Grack
Harry Viola
Dick Voehl

Larry Wassong
Margerie Weissman
Irene Weitzenkorn
Judy West

Carin Zakes

## Chicago Office

Diane Cary
Steve Rhea

## Los Angeles Office

John Killpack

## Yellow Pages Division

Ed Andrich
Linda Call-Traush
John Hughes
Jim Kline
Ed Kovach
Sandy Kovach
Arlene Taylor
Marilyn Viers

# BIOGRAPHIES

## Marc Wyse

Born the son of European immigrants, Marc Wyse grew up a happy child in the vibrant and ethnic Kinsman neighborhood of Cleveland. He displayed his unique combination of athletic, academic, journalistic and people prowess at John Adams High School and went on to Western Reserve University. He took a diversion to Dartmouth College, where he studied with Robert Frost, returning to Western Reserve to complete his degree in English, all the while planning to launch his own business.

Just a few years after graduating, Marc co-founded Wyse Advertising in downtown Cleveland with little in his pocket and big ideas in his head. As they say, the rest is history. Marc went on to become one of the premier advertising CEOs in America, with a client list that featured American Greetings Corp., BP America, Clairol, Gimbel's, Sherwin-Williams, Smucker's, and Stouffer's Frozen Foods. Wyse Advertising remained one of the top advertising agencies in the U.S. for several decades, winning countless awards every year. The firm was famous for developing the classic slogan for the J. M. Smucker Co. — "With a name like Smucker's, it has to be good." — that provided Smucker's with national brand recognition.

In his memoirs, Marc reveals his diligence and drive to achieve excellence combined with the fun that he experienced in his role as energetic entrepreneur who encouraged his employees to excel, as they grew Wyse Advertising into one of the most prominent and successful agencies. The worldly Wyse provides astute and often humorous business and life lessons and inspiring stories of the celebrities and luminaries he met along the way, including Arnold Palmer, Bill Cosby, Bill Gates, Ginger Rogers and Carl Stokes.

Marc lived in Cleveland with his wife Sheila. He had three children, Jennifer, Robert, and Katherine, and five grandchildren. Marc died at the age of 88 in July 2011. He led his life with passion, humor, grace and kindness to all.

## Christopher Johnston

Christopher Johnston has worked as a Cleveland-based journalist and author since 1987. He has published more than 3,000 articles in regional and national publications. He also wrote and edited four memoir books with Frederick C. Crawford, founding chairman of TRW Inc. His website is www.ChristopherJohnstonWriter.com

## Dan Fauver

Dan Fauver was one of Marc Wyse's art directors (and Vice President & Associate Creative Director) for over 30 years. He came to Wyse in 1977 via Meldrum & Fewsmith Advertising, Exit Magazine and Cleveland Magazine. He's won hundreds of awards for Marc's retail, industrial and corporate clients. Many of his ads have been translated into 18 different languages. Dan now works from an office at Melamed Riley Advertising on PlayhouseSquare in Cleveland. Some sample ads, his long list of client experience and contact info can be found at DanFauver.com.

The Wyse Advertising lobby on the fourth floor at 2800 Euclid welcomed visitors with weathered barn-wood walls that were adeptly appointed with antique advertising posters and artifacts from the 19th and early 20th centuries.